Codependency Recovery Guide

A Woman's Guide to Stop Being Codependent, Find Inner Freedom and Never Be Needy Again

Linda Hill

Table of Contents

Your Secret Gift #1

Get My Next Book

"Codependency Recovery Guide - Part 2"

(Free for a limited time)

For a limited time, and as a "Thank you" for purchasing this book, you can be added to our "Book 2 Launch List" for free so you get the second book of this series when it gets published (This book will be priced at $24.99 and I guarantee it will be a great read). Simply visit the URL below and follow the instructions. You'll be the first to get it.

Visit here:

lindahillbooks.com/crg

Scan QR Code:

Your Secret Gift #2

Get the Audio Version for Free

If you would like to get the audio version of this book so you can read along or listen while you are in the car, walking around, or doing other things, you're in luck. For a limited time, I've provided a link that will allow you to download this audiobook for FREE. (This offer may be removed at any time).

Step 1: Go to the URL below.

Step 2: Sign up for the 30-day free-trial membership (You may cancel at any time after, no strings attached)

Step 3: Listen to the audiobook

Visit here:

lindahillbooks.com/crgpromo

Scan QR Code:

Introduction

The most important reason for going from one place to another is to see what's in between, and they took great pleasure in doing just that.

—Norton Juster

In the modern world, many women have become increasingly protective of their individuality and lifestyle; and just as many women have developed a fear of entering a romantic relationship. You yourself may fall into one of these two categories. While neither are necessarily bad—especially as it's a personal choice—you may make this decision because you find it difficult to enter a romantic relationship without losing who you are in the process. A woman is called "codependent," according to Khoshaba (2013), when she enters into relationships and attaches herself in a dependent manner to her partner, a friend, family member, food, or substance—like alcohol or drugs—to satisfy unmet physical and emotional needs that originated from her childhood.

Growing up in a home where one or more family members displayed codependent tendencies puts you at risk of growing up to become a codependent adult. As such, codependency is often cyclical, meaning it is passed down from past generations. Behaviors linked to codependency often occur in environments that face challenges and experienced stressors like abuse, addiction, or mental illness. It's difficult for you to learn how to cultivate a healthy relationship with your partner, friends, and family members as an adult when you grew up in a dysfunctional home environment. For many of the women who grew up this way, it becomes more difficult for them to live an independent lifestyle. As a result, codependency has been found to share traits with mental disorders like depression, post-traumatic stress disorder (PTSD), and obsessive-compulsive behavior (OCD) (Hull, 2022).

Originally, "codependency" was a term that was used to refer to the relationship that a person had with a substance (like alcohol or drugs); however, in the present, "codependency" covers a broader range of behaviors and relationships. As a life coach who helps and guides people who want to escape from unhealthy relationships, I aim to teach you what codependency is, where it comes from, how it impacts your life, and how you can recover from codependency and codependent relationships. Once you have read through this book and completed the activities, you will have learned how to love yourself, care for the woman that you have become, and cultivate and maintain your independence so that you can start your journey to recovery. Each chapter will build on the other, creating a foundation that aims to help you be the woman that you really are, and care for her and her future without losing yourself again.

What Will I Cover?

I will begin by teaching you what codependency really is and how it looks for women. This will provide you with the foundation needed for the chapters that follow. You will learn how and why codependency develops, as well as how it often originates from your childhood. It's important that you understand how codependency originates so that you can gain a better understanding of how your mind works. This will help you understand the impact that codependency has on your self-esteem, how it encourages feelings of shame and guilt, and promotes people-pleasing behavior. You may feel apprehensive about delving into the psychology behind codependency, but it provides important information that will help you understand why many of the relationships in your life—whether they are familial, friendly, or romantic—are codependent in nature.

Codependent relationships have a tendency to promote feelings of resentment. You might not even be aware of such feelings, but that doesn't mean that they aren't there. Caring for others and giving them everything that you are without receiving the smallest bit of appreciation is hard. It can wear you down, which is why it's important to identify when you are both mentally and physically exhausted. As a result, self-care becomes an important part of the recovery process. Taking care of yourself isn't as glamorous as the media thinks it is. Self-care involves setting boundaries, practicing mindfulness so that you can notice when old habits start to reappear, and even going to therapy. It's a strategy that helps you take care of yourself as you go through the recovery process.

Nurturing the woman that you have been protecting all your life will involve picturing what you want your life to look like weeks, months, and even years from now. But remember, your success will come from staying consistent and committed to your journey. It will take patience, hard work, and consistent practice—even on your bad days. You will face challenges during your journey, that's normal. It's important that you don't allow these challenges to hold you back. While I can't account for every possible challenge you may face during your recovery, I will cover the common issues that women recovering from codependency face—like self-sabotage and relapse—and how to overcome them.

As a woman recovering from codependency, it's important that you start learning how to love and care for yourself before pursuing future romantic relationships. Essentially, you need to date yourself and learn how to love the woman that you are, without any conditions, before you can start dating other people and developing healthy relationships with them. This will help you avoid repeating codependent behaviors and tendencies in future relationships, which is an important step to maintaining your independence. Learning how to be independent will teach you how to be interdependent once you do enter a relationship. This involves learning how to receive and accept love, gifts, and other acts of service that are found in a healthy relationship.

Upon completion of this book, you will have the ability to identify if you have codependent tendencies, how they impact you, the different strategies that you can use to cope with leaving a codependent relationship, how to put them into practice, as well as how to create a recovery process that will benefit you for years to come.

What Will You Need?

- a notebook to write in, complete activities, track your progress and thinking

- a pen to write with

- colored pencils

- your cell phone's timer

Call to Action

As women, we all lead different lives and have experienced unique hardships. However, many of us miss out on our lives because of our codependent tendencies and relationships. You don't have to be ashamed of your codependency because many women are struggling with similar challenges. But it's time for you to make a change in your life so that you can move forward and start recovering. Take your first step to freedom and move onto Chapter 1.

CHAPTER 1

The Symptoms of a Codependent Woman

Other people's lives, problems, and wants set the course for my life. Once I realized it was okay for me to think about and identify what I wanted, remarkable things began to take place in my life.

–Melody Beattie

When the needs of a young girl are not adequately met, she is at risk of growing up to become a codependent woman. Unmet physical and emotional needs encourage these women to rely on others to have their needs met. This drive gives her two options: She can either give in and allow herself to rely solely on others to meet her needs, or she can rely on herself by building an independent lifestyle that is self-sufficient and protects her from relationships that could put her emotional safety at risk. To start your journey, you have to understand what codependency is and how it manifests in your daily life so that you can identify whether or not you have codependency.

What Is Codependency?

According to the Merriam-Webster dictionary (n.d.), "codependency" is a psychological condition where a woman with low self-esteem, and a desire for approval, develops a dependent relationship with another person (a family member, friend, or romantic partner who displays controlling or manipulative behavior) or to a thing (like food, alcohol, medication, or drugs). As you work through this book, it's important that you remember that while codependency has many common traits and behaviors, it will look different for everyone.

Our attachment style is developed during childhood, providing the opportunity for codependent behaviors to manifest as we grow up. This style of attachment can result in dysfunctional relationship dynamics that may encourage you to depend on your partner, family member, or friend physically, mentally, and spiritually, with an all-consuming and unhealthy reliance. Such relationships often experience additional problems like abuse, addiction, and mental illness. In a codependent relationship, you can take on one of two roles: the giver or the taker. The giver sacrifices their needs and well-being for the benefit of the taker. The taker doesn't provide the giver with anything in return (no appreciation, care, support, or love).

When a woman takes on the role of the giver in her relationship, she may start to underestimate herself and feel less confident about who she is due to a lack of self-esteem. Instead, she begins to idealize the taker, believing that they're smarter and more worthy than she is. The survival of the giver becomes dependent on their ability to suppress their physical and emotional needs in order to give the taker what they appear to need. This is draining work! Over time, you start to lose yourself to your relationship, giving up your identity to keep the taker in your life. You may not even realize that you have lost yourself until you begin asking questions like, "What do I like to do?" or, "What's my favorite food?"

Activity: Take a moment to answer these two questions in your notebook. Reflect on your answers and determine if your answers were influenced by your partner's choices.

You may be looking for someone or something to blame as you start your recovery journey. However, the best thing that you can do is to avoid blaming or guilting yourself for being codependent. Honestly, it can happen to anyone, especially when you have experienced trauma. The most important part of starting your journey to recovery is to acknowledge and accept the fact that you are codependent or have codependent tendencies. Whether you have taken up the role of giver or taker in your relationship, you have to decide if you are finally going to take the first step to recovering from codependency so that you can create a better, healthier life for yourself. To start this process, you have to understand the different types of codependency that you may be experiencing.

Types of Codependency

Codependency can take on different forms. If you suspect that you have codependent tendencies, use the following codependent categories to help you determine the type of codependent woman that you could be. You may even fall into more than one group. In your notebook, note the codependent classification that you identify with, including the characteristics of this category, so that you can start noticing these signs in your daily life.

- **Passive:** A fear of conflict means that you will do what you can to avoid it. If you are unable to avoid conflict, you may start to dissociate. Dissociation normally occurs when a woman has experienced trauma in the past. Instead of giving in to your anger and resentment, you adopt an empathetic, compassionate, and generous façade. This is because you learned from your initial trauma that fighting back can result in more serious consequences, so it becomes a defense mechanism that keeps you safe.

- **Active:** Some women take on a more active role in their codependent relationship. They may attempt to manipulate their partner into loving and respecting them by using techniques like counter-aggression, constant vigilance, and surveillance of their partner. However, this confrontational and aggressive approach can harm both members of the relationship.

- **Cerebral:** When a woman experiences abuse by a narcissistic partner, she may believe that if she continues to learn and gather knowledge, she will be able to solve the problems in her codependent relationship. However, this won't heal the trauma that she has suffered.

- **Oblivious:** A defense mechanism used by codependent women to protect themselves. This mechanism helps her remain comfortable in her relationship by not acknowledging the trauma, abuse, or the dysfunction that she experiences in her relationship.

- **Anorexic:** It's possible that a woman may decide to completely surrender to her codependent relationship with a narcissistic partner. Surrendering is a mechanism that can help her feel safe, but it also denies her the healthy physical and emotional intimacy that is important for her overall well-being.

Symptoms of Codependency

Many of the symptoms of codependency are natural feelings experienced by everyone; however, when these feelings start to **consume** you, you can lose your identity as a woman and your sense of self-worth. This loss could indicate that you are codependent. Using the following list, make a note of the symptoms that you have experienced, or identify with, in your notebook. While the list that follows is not a diagnostic tool, a high number of these symptoms may indicate that you could have codependent tendencies. According to Selva (2018) and Gould (2020), the symptoms of codependency include

- low self-esteem

- narcissism

- familial dysfunction

- a constant need to check in with your partner or friend

- poor emotional expressivity

- trouble saying "no"

- an inability to ask for help

- needing permission to do daily tasks

- depression

- trouble taking time for yourself

- feeling as though you don't know who you when you're on your own

- anxiety

- a tendency to apologize even if you didn't do anything wrong

- stress

- lack of boundaries

- a compulsion to care for others

- needing to be in control

- difficulty making your own decisions

- difficulty communicating honestly

- fixating on mistakes

- a constant need to be in a relationship

- having a need to be liked by others

- doing things for the other person even if these tasks make you uncomfortable

- issues with intimacy

- taking responsibility for the other person or taking on their responsibilities

- trouble accepting your feelings, thoughts, and emotions

- confusing love for pity

- constantly feeling sorry for the other individual

- a fear of abandonment

Codependency Is Unhealthy

In a healthy relationship, you will be able to rely on your partner to provide you with the same amount of love, care, support, and protection that they receive from you. In other words, your relationship has a mutually beneficial dynamic. However, in a codependent relationship, the giving of love and support is normally one-sided. This means that one person is putting in all the work in the relationship while their partner receives all the benefits.

For example, Jen provided her partner Alfred with help, support, love, and care for the past two years that they have been dating. During this time, Jen gave Alfred everything that she thought he needed—even if he didn't actually need it—by taking on the role of the giver in their relationship. Alfred was quite content with taking all that Jen offered him without giving anything in return. Their relationship was codependent. In such a relationship, the destructive behavior of the taker—Alfred's gambling addiction—may be inadvertently encouraged by the giver. Unfortunately, Jen's reliability and caring nature meant that she neglected herself during these two years. Her relationship with Alfred gave her poor self-esteem, encouraged people-pleasing behavior, and made it difficult for her to reinforce her boundaries.

In this scenario, Jen's giving tendencies meant that she ended up paying the money that Alfred owed on his gambling debts. When Jen started to create an emotional distance between herself and Alfred, before moving to end their relationship, Alfred was exposed to the consequences of his addictive behavior. He had to pay his own gambling debts and start taking care of himself. As such, emotional distance may force the taker to finally take responsibility for their behavior and solve their problems without the giver taking on the burden for them.

This is only one possible scenario of a codependent relationship. Every woman's experience is different. Your experience may be more or less extreme than Jen's. But the point of the scenario is to show you that a codependent relationship is unhealthy. I'm not telling you to avoid relationships or never care for anyone else. Our emotions are not a weakness, but what I'm trying to demonstrate is that when you have an addiction to an unhealthy relationship—whether you realize it or not—your caring and nurturing behavior can become unhealthy and harm both members of the relationship. This can result in abusive, emotionally destructive, and one-sided relationships that are harmful to you and may result in you losing your identity and sense of self-worth. Although it's important to have the ability to identify whether you have codependent tendencies, you also need to know the signs of a codependent relationship.

Signs of a Codependent Relationship

During the course of your life, you develop relationships with family members, friends, romantic partners, and even things like food, alcohol, or drugs (both legal and illegal). Codependency is not limited to a romantic relationship or a substance, which is why it's important to be able to identify the signs of a codependent relationship. According to WebMD Editorial Contributors (2020), the six signs below may indicate that you are in a codependent relationship. As you move through this section, reflect on your relationships with your partner (past or present), friends, family members, food, and substances. Use your reflection to identify whether you have been in, or are currently in, a codependent relationship.

Paying Compulsive Attention to Someone

An ever-present need to remain connected to the other person in your relationship because you feel as though you can't live without them. This may prevent you from feeling comfortable around them because you are afraid that if they knew the real you, they would leave.

Fear of Abandonment

Building on the above characteristic, fear that your partner will leave you may cause you to alter your behavior in a way that will convince them to stay. You might start to conceal how you really feel or lie to your partner, losing your real self in the process.

A Lack of External Support Systems

Relying solely on your partner leaves you with little time to cultivate and maintain relationships with family and friends. You lose a healthy and valuable external support system, as well as people that are important to you because your focus is solely on your partner.

Enmeshed Sense of Shame

When you are dependent on another person, you may feel as though your entire personality revolves around them, this makes it difficult to know who you *actually* are. This can induce feelings of guilt and shame.

Self-Doubt

Focusing on your partner and staking your identity on them negatively impacts your self-esteem and ability to make decisions. You start doubting yourself and would prefer that others make decisions for you. Additionally, you don't know who you are as an individual anymore.

Resentment

The unhealthy dynamic found in a codependent relationship may cause you to resent your partner, while also feeling as though you cannot live without them. These two emotions might clash with each other, but their negative impact remains the same.

Key Takeaways

- Codependency originates from your childhood attachment styles.

- Low self-esteem and an intense desire for approval contribute to codependency.

- Codependent relationships are not mutually beneficial. As such, the "taker" never shows appreciation for the "giver."

- It's important to not blame yourself for your codependency. Rather, you should focus on recognizing and acknowledging your codependent behaviors.

- The symptoms of codependency originate from normal emotions that become so intense that they consume you, affecting you negatively.

- Codependency is unhealthy because it consumes your identity, encouraging people-pleasing behavior, poor self-esteem, as well as making it difficult to reinforce your boundaries.

Reflective Activity

Answer the following questions in your notebook to help you reflect on your childhood and identify possible signs of codependency.

1. Did your parents demonstrate codependent or narcissistic

behavior when you were a child?

2. How did their behavior impact you?

3. What did you feel while reading this chapter? Shocked, angry, relieved, or maybe guilty? Allo

4. w yourself to acknowledge and feel these emotions, but don't act on them or allow them to consume you.

5. Did you have to take responsibility for yourself when you were a child?

6. As an adult, have you had to parent yourself? Take time to reflect on your adulthood before answering this question.

7. Reflecting on your past and current relationships, describe whether you had to play the role of "parent."

CHAPTER 2

It's Not Your Fault, It Was Your Childhood Trauma

Forgive yourself for the survival patterns and traits you picked up while enduring trauma.
–Audrey Kitching

Sometimes, a situation may be perceived as traumatic by one person, while the other person deems the situation as normal or acceptable. As such, "trauma" is used to describe a person's intense emotional response to a specific situation or event that they perceive to be a threat to their safety and well-being; or it triggers intense negative emotions like fear, pain, worry, and grief. In such situations, you may feel powerless or hopeless, adding to the negative feelings you are already experiencing. When you grow up in a family that dismisses and ignores their members' emotions, codependency can take root.

Examples of some common traumatic situations include

experiencing natural disasters, losing a person or animal that you love, experiencing physical or emotional abuse, witnessing abuse or violence, assault of any kind, or being involved in combat scenarios (whether you were a soldier or a civilian). While this list isn't exhaustive, each situation has two things in common: Intense negative emotions triggered by a threat to your physical and emotional safety, and their consequences. Traumatic situations trigger our fight, flight, freeze, and fawn response. This is a common survival response to traumatic situations and experiences, and it aims to keep you safe. According to Sosnoski (2021), the four common survival responses to trauma include:

- **Fight:** When you react in an aggressive, physical or verbal manner to something that you perceive to be a threat.

- **Flight:** Takes the shape of overworking yourself or using substances, like alcohol, to avoid a situation that you perceive to be a threat.

- **Freeze:** When you dissociate or distract yourself from a situation that makes you feel threatened. It can take the form of daydreaming, watching television, scrolling through social media, or working long hours without being asked.

- **Fawn:** When the other trauma responses fail to work, you may accept the abuse and flatter or manipulate your abuser to try and make the abuse stop. Essentially, fawn is a survival mechanism that you developed in response to a traumatic experience.

The consequences of your trauma can manifest as codependent behavior, as well as problems with your physical and emotional health. Addictive tendencies can also develop. You may use legal and illegal substances (like alcohol and drugs) as a coping mechanism, but you can heal from your trauma. It isn't easy and it takes time, but it is possible. First, you have to identify where your codependency originates from. It can be difficult for you to accept and acknowledge the trauma that resulted in your codependency. Denial is normal when you have memories and experiences that you would prefer to forget. However, you should not give up as soon as you encounter an obstacle on your journey to recovery. Take a deep breath, allow yourself to acknowledge your feelings, but keep your momentum and continue moving forwards. It took strength to get to this point in your life where you are looking to help yourself, so don't give up.

Childhood Trauma and Its Influence on Codependency

You may find that while you want to help yourself, you also find it difficult to accept that there is an issue. It's difficult to accept that you may have a problem, especially when this acknowledgement means that you lose the control you have carefully cultivated to keep yourself safe, but if you give in to this denial instead of working past it, you will continue to be impacted by your emotions, struggle with any form of intimacy, or obsess over and remain addicted to your relationships. To move forward on your journey to recovery, you need to understand the origins of your codependency. In the previous chapter, I briefly mentioned how your childhood trauma can be responsible for your codependency.

Childhood Trauma

When we are children, we depend on the adults around us to provide for us, meet our needs, and give us the love, affection, acceptance, and approval that we need to grow up into functional adults. If you experience trauma as a child, this is often not what happens. You already know that trauma has a lasting impact that can manifest as codependent behaviors as you grow up. While it isn't necessarily healthy, it does make sense. When you are a child, you don't have the tools, resources, or experience to cope like an adult would in that same situation. As a result, codependency often stems from the trauma that you experienced when you were a child. This trauma can include, but isn't limited to, domestic violence, divorce, neglect, abuse, and fighting by those who live in your home (this could include your parents, aunts, uncles, grandparents, and even siblings fighting). Essentially, the trauma in your childhood that causes codependency will normally revolve around your family, their behavior and their response to each other and a situation.

You may not realize it as a child, but such an environment can make you feel mentally and physically unsafe. Feelings of helplessness and a need to rely on others starts to develop. As you grow up, you feel the need for other people to fulfill your emotional needs and validate you because, as a child, you were unable to develop the skills needed to do it yourself. You struggle to feel confident in who you are as an individual. This can also be connected to your lack of positive role models as you grew up. I think one of the hardest parts of your journey to recovery will be reflecting on your childhood and identifying your trauma, acknowledging how it impacted you and made you feel, but still deciding to move forwards—toward recovery—instead of allowing it to consume you.

It's hard to look back on your childhood and realize that it wasn't as great as you thought it was, but don't dismiss your good memories or experiences, either. You did what you could to survive and get to where you are today. Frankly, you need to celebrate your continued resilience and survival. Now it's time to move forwards because that traumatized young girl grew up into a woman who needs you. Make the decision to be there for her, to show yourself compassion, and allow yourself to move forward with your life in a healthier and more positive manner.

The Traumatized Child Who Became a Codependent Woman

When you are a codependent adult, you are at risk of—or are currently—depending on other people to validate and praise you, as well as fulfill your emotional needs. This creates a coping mechanism, known as "trauma bonding," that makes it difficult for you to break free from abuse and heal from your trauma. Don't let it discourage you. It's merely an obstacle on your journey that you'll be able to overcome with hard work, patience, and perseverance.

It's normal for human beings to want to attach themselves to other people; however, your childhood trauma can cause trauma bonding. "Trauma bonding" is an unhealthy attachment style that has the potential to become harmful to both members of a relationship, whether the relationship is romantic, friendly, or familial. The harm caused by trauma bonding can be emotional or physical; however, it becomes difficult for a woman who experiences trauma bonding to leave a harmful relationship because you develop an "addiction" to your partner. Basically, you feel like you cannot live without your partner because you have a responsibility to fix them.

When you are a codependent woman in an abusive relationship

—whether you are an adult or a child—your feelings and behaviors toward your abuser often develop from your inaccurate sense of reality because you don't know that this type of relationship isn't normal. Feelings like pity may be confused with love for your abuser. You truly believe that your partner will finally change; however, you also struggle to manage your negative feelings toward them. In a codependent relationship, your focus is solely on your partner. It becomes difficult for you to set healthy boundaries and actively reinforce them when your partner crosses them, allowing them to manipulate and control you. In a healthy relationship, your partner would not be taking advantage of your difficulty to set boundaries.

While you cannot change the past that created your codependency, you can change your emotional response to past and present trauma. This is important. While trauma negatively impacts you, your emotional response to it has the ability to alter its impact on your emotional and mental well-being. The first step to catering your emotional response is to understand your codependent tendencies better. After all, you can't solve $x + 2 = 4$ without x. This math concept from our time at school applies to managing your emotional response. You have to understand how your codependency impacts your life so that you can permanently recover from it.

Affirmation Activity: In your notebook, write down the following phrase, "I can't change the past and that's okay." You may struggle to accept this statement at first, but it's important that when intrusive thoughts and memories start to appear in your mind, making you wish you could change the past, you repeat the above statement. This phrase works like an affirmation. You won't believe it at first, but over time you will start to accept and believe that the past cannot be changed, and it really is okay. Unfortunately, we don't have a time machine that can take us back to the past so that we can protect our younger selves.

The neglect and abuse that you experience as a child are the most common causes of post-traumatic stress disorder (PTSD) and attachment disorders like codependency. I've already discussed how as a child, you lack the resources and skills to be able to effectively cope with such trauma. As a result, you blame yourself for the trauma that you experienced, even though your parents or caretakers are the ones who should be blamed for neglecting their responsibility to you. Childhood trauma has been recognized for creating two different outcomes: It either helps you become more resilient, or you struggle to develop into an independent woman who has a stable sense of self. This can explain why a codependent woman will be more prone to entering a relationship with a person who will reassure them that they were a victim, or a relationship where their partner needs them to accept responsibility for actions and behaviors that are not their own.

Examples of such relationships include a partner who calls in sick for their spouse who spent the night drinking and is too hungover (or still drunk) to go to work, a parent that excuses and hides their child's harmful behavior, or an employee who takes responsibility for their manager's inappropriate behavior at work. You may have even experienced similar situations yourself. As a child, unhealthy relationships, like those discussed above, may encourage you to take on a specific role in your family dynamic.

The Family Roles Created by Trauma

In families where children are affected by trauma, four family roles are created. Read through the following list of roles and write down the family role that you identify with the most. If you identify with more than one role, include it in your notes. This will help you identify the type of codependent behaviors you may take part in. According to Dahansi (2020), these roles include the:

- **Family hero:** This role is normally taken on by the oldest child. The oldest child believes that they need to be perfect, so they do their best to be as responsible as possible. They will also act as the family's protector.

- **Lost child:** Normally taken on by the middle or youngest child, this role helps the child attract the least amount of attention from their parents. They normally follow the lead of others. Some general traits of this role include partaking in hobbies that involve an element of fantasy. They are often thought of as the loners of the family, but they aren't disruptive either. As adults, they suffer from depression and anxiety, fear intimacy, and aren't prone to taking risks.

- **Scapegoat:** Generally, the rebellious, antisocial, and troubled child is the second born child who is often the focus of their parent's rage. Whenever something goes wrong in their parents' life, they blame this child. Blame may take the form of emotional or physical abuse.

- **Mascot or clown:** The youngest child who is often protected by their parents. They always try to make everyone else laugh. They use jokes to ease the tension between family members and in the home environment. However, this child is normally deeply insecure and anxious. As adults, they may self-medicate and are more prone to becoming addicts.

Once you have identified your role in your family as a child, you can identify whether the person you are right now is your authentic or false self. This will help you understand just how much of your true self you have lost to codependency. It will help you to determine what techniques could effectively help you on your journey to recovery.

- **Authentic self:** When you are able to actively work toward becoming the unique woman you really are. You stop craving others' lives, and your existence no longer revolves around the happiness of others or their validation of you. You are free to make your own choices because your energy is no longer being spent on appeasing and controlling others. You start feeling less angry at life and begin to feel more alive.

- **False self:** The version of us that is created to protect our authentic self. She is the woman who became what you needed to be to survive; however, this often means losing your authentic self in the process. But you can find her again!

The Parentified Child

Growing up in a dysfunctional home where you were exposed to abuse or trauma creates an experience that is known as "non-parenting." It's a lethal form of abuse that involves your parents neglecting or ignoring you when you were a child. However, just as with identifying your trauma, it can take time, patience, and hard work to identify this type of parenting in your childhood.

Especially because children who suffered the form of abuse believe that they only imagined it. Children are sensitive and pick up on everything. When the adults in their lives are physically worn out or emotionally fragile, the children notice it and may feel responsible and helpless. This creates a codependent relationship that creates a perpetuating cycle where codependency is passed down between the generations. If you are a woman who was subjected to this type of generational dysfunction, you may start to realize that the way you form relationships, solve problems, and view yourself is identical to how your parents and grandparents performed these behaviors. You need to actively decide to make and implement the changes needed to recover.

As a child who experiences non-parenting, you are forced to take on your parents' responsibilities. Essentially, you become the parent. This is known as the "parentified child." While you are busy taking care of your parents, siblings, yourself, the chores, paying bills, or cooking, your parents are behaving like children. They may even try and sabotage your caretaking efforts, only adding to the stress that you are already experiencing. The parentified child can be any gender and age, but this role is usually taken on by the oldest or middle child. Parentification is common in families where parents suffer from severe mental illness or addiction, are emotionally immature, do not have a basic understanding of child development and safety, or understand how their behavior will impact their children.

How Parentification Effects You

According to Martin (2020), the human brain is not fully developed until our mid–20s. As a result, being a child who has to take on the responsibility of adulthood and parenting without the maturity, experience, or resources needed is extremely stressful, tiring, and even traumatic. The lack of role models in such a situation makes it even more difficult for you to cope. You are a child who is trying to understand your emotions, trauma, and experiences of growing up, and now you also have to manage a home and care for parents who are actively working against you. You lack the guidance that every child needs, causing you to feel alone, overwhelmed, scared, and angry. You are forced to give up friends, goals, interests, and your childhood to care for those responsible for you.

Entering adulthood after being a parentified child can create challenges like increased mental health issues, compulsive caretaking, trouble trusting other people, high levels of anxiety, feelings of inadequacy and loneliness, losing yourself in your work, perfectionism, trouble setting boundaries, and a loss of your true identity. You deny your needs and feelings because you don't believe that they matter. This impacts your mental and physical health even further. It becomes difficult for you to stand up for yourself, feel confident, or pursue your goals.

An Introduction to the Recovery Process

You are not responsible for the development of your codependency; however, you have to put in the work to recover from it. Break the healing process down into smaller steps that you can easily manage. This takes some of the fear that accompanies change away. Recovery from codependency is best explained using Jeanette Elisabeth Menter's "hierarchy of survival" that is found in her book *You're Not Crazy—You're Codependent: What Everyone Affected By Addiction, Abuse, Trauma, or Toxic Shaming Must Know to Have Peace in Their Lives* (Dahansi, 2020). Menter was a survivor of childhood abuse, addiction, and shaming. Her book aims to teach readers about codependency and how it uses self-sabotage to control you. She explains that through finding the truth, you can find freedom. Menter's hierarchy of enlightenment was explained by Duhansi (2020), as follows:

- As you go on your journey of recovery, you are first too afraid and isolated to know any other way of living your life that doesn't solely involve your survival.

- You start to become aware that this isn't a normal way to live, but you don't know anything else. This can be a painful realization to know that there is another, safer way of living.

- Now you begin looking for help from others and different sources so that you can change your circumstances. When you reach this point, you will understand what you have to do to recover; however, you have not begun to physically implement these changes yet. As such, real transformation has not yet occurred.

- In the final step, your mind, spirit, and body connect. This connection allows you to see the way out of a codependent life and helps you to actively move toward implementing the changes needed to achieve it, allowing you to embrace your authentic self.

Codependency recovery involves healing from the childhood trauma that caused it. When you are shamed, ignored, or punished for expressing your thoughts and feelings, not allowed to be immature or imperfect, or told that you cannot have needs and wants, your mental health and well-being is negatively impacted. You come to the conclusion that if you cannot rely on other people, then you cannot trust them either. You protect yourself by hiding your inner child and putting on an adult disguise. But this can be extremely harmful to your well-being, development, and ability to cope, creating wounds that scar over as you grow up. Healing means looking at your scars, opening them up to clean them properly, and then treating them with medication to help you heal properly.

According to Dahunsi (2020), in order to heal from your childhood trauma and make a positive change in your life, you need to make four different commitments.

- Set aside a specific amount of time everyday to work on improving your well-being.

- Give yourself permission to look at who you are from a new perspective. When you have spent your life not seeing who you truly are, this can give you a distorted view about the person you believe yourself to be.

- Prepare yourself to move from understanding what you need to do, to actively implementing these positive changes. Remember that everyone is unique! As such, there is no right or wrong way for you to make this change in your life.

- Don't allow your guilt over the past and present to consume you. Be unmoving in your belief that you will become a healthy woman who has taken control of her life and will be true to herself.

Key Takeaways

- Trauma looks different for everyone.

- Your fight, flight, freeze, or fawn response will be triggered in response to a dangerous situation.

- Codependency originates from childhood trauma.

- This can manifest as trauma bonding that will impact you as an adult.

- The different family roles created by trauma will impact your identity and sense of self.

- The parentified child is created when parents ignore their responsibilities to their children and their lives.

- Parentification can severely impact the trauma you already experienced during your childhood.

- You can recover from your childhood trauma.

Reflective Activity

Using the information in this chapter, reflect on your childhood and answer the questions that follow in your notebook.

1. Reflect on and identify how your parents treated you as a child.

2. How did their treatment make you feel when you were a child and now as an adult?

3. Can you recognize instances of trauma, like abuse and neglect, from your childhood?

4. Name three effects of your childhood trauma on you as an adult.

5. Did you ever have to take responsibility for any members of your family as a child?

6. How did this responsibility impact you?

Chapter 3

"I Need You to Need Me"

Dignity will only happen when you realize that having someone in your life doesn't validate your worth.
–Shannon L. Alder

Our family and the environment that we grew up in interact like a system. As you grew up, this system developed in a way that ensured its continued survival. The system's survival depended on its spoken and unspoken rules. If you didn't follow these rules, or accidentally broke them, you would face negative consequences. These rules did not cater to the unique needs and wants of each member in this system. Problems such as addiction, mental illness, neglect, and abuse may have resulted from members trying to cope with the rules.

Rules that were put in place to preserve the system, at the expense of its members' well-being, creates the perfect environment for the development of codependent behavior and relationships. As children of this system grow up, they are denied the freedom that they need to develop in a healthy manner. Instead, children hide their true identity so that they can become who they need to be to survive. This results in a loss of self-worth, self-concept, self-esteem, and confidence to name a few. As codependent adults, these women find it difficult to separate their reality from the reality of the system that they grew up in, creating behavior that does not match who these women really are. Therefore, to find your true self, you need to understand the mind of a woman who is codependent.

The Psychology of a Codependent Woman

Women who grew up in a family with abusive and neglectful parents have a higher risk of becoming codependent adults; however, everyone is at risk of developing a codependent relationship. I need you to remember that while many sources and books are referring to romantic relationships, a codependent relationship can develop between friends, family members, and even in the work environment. This is due to the fact that women who are empathetic, caring, have a giving nature, and are focused on other people—in addition to their childhood trauma and upbringing—are at a higher risk of developing codependent tendencies and relationships (Burn, 2017).

Traditional feminine roles occur when women take on the role of daughter, sister, niece, wife, daughter-in-law, mother, and grandmother. Female gender roles dictate that characteristics like giving, helping, caring, and nurturing are traits that define a woman. As women, we don't even realize that we are taking part in these roles because such traits and behaviors are considered normal. Unfortunately, we may have a tendency to be excessive when fulfilling the role of "giver." You may not even notice that you are doing it. According to Burns (2017), excessive helping and giving behaviors that become unhealthy are deemed as normal when you are a woman. Women are often encouraged by society and their culture to perform such behaviors in order to correctly fulfill their expected feminine roles. We are expected to put other people first, always be polite and friendly, and be considerate toward others before thinking about our own needs and wants. As young girls, many of us are taught and encouraged to care for everyone else at the expense of our own well-being because being "selfless" is considered an ideal trait, even if it hurts us.

However, excessive giving behavior and tendencies can negatively impact your mental, physical, and spiritual well-being. You may also find that your relationships—with family members, friends, and romantic partners—are unbalanced. This means that your giving behavior enables the other person's poor functioning, protects them from the consequences of their actions and decisions, and it may drain your physical and mental energy, while depleting your material resources, leaving nothing for you to use when you need it. Gender roles, society, and many cultures may also promote the idea that women should sacrifice who they are to "selflessly" care for others. We may not even realize that our own families are promoting these roles, ideals, and values.

There is nothing wrong with you if you unconsciously partake in these behaviors. It also does not mean that caring, helping, nurturing, and giving behaviors are bad. In fact, they can be great traits to have. What I am trying to get across is that when you excessively perform these behaviors, to the point that you start to suffer, then they can start becoming harmful—to you and the people around you—even if you didn't intend for your behavior to be harmful.

In the last chapter, I explained that you can't change the past and that point is important here as well. Don't allow your past behaviors and actions consume you. Yes, you may feel guilty or anxious, but don't lose yourself to these emotions. Acknowledge and accept them, then move forwards. Look at where you currently are in life and decide where you want to be. Now, make a plan to get there. As a codependent woman, you may currently be at a place where you are sacrificing who you are for others, but you want to reach the point where you have the ability to care for yourself and others without hurting or losing your identity in the process. The first thing you need to do, after completing the activities in the last two chapters, is to identify your pattern of codependency.

The Patterns of Codependency

According to Jones (2020), there are five common patterns of codependency that a woman may perform in her daily life and relationships. These patterns consist of a variety of characteristics and behaviors that help her to protect herself from being hurt by her partner and cope with the negative feelings that accompany codependency. In your notebook, write down the pattern(s) that you identify with. Note the specific characteristics of each pattern that you have performed in your daily life. This activity will help you to actively take notice of these patterns as you go about your day.

Denial

When you follow a pattern of denial, you may find it difficult to identify your own feelings. This may even cause you to minimize and alter how you really feel about a person, situation, or experience, while perceiving yourself to be selfless and dedicated to the well-being of the people in your life—whether they are a friend, family member, coworker, partner, or acquaintance.

Avoidance

When a behavior or action could incite rejection, anger, or shame from other people, you may perform avoidance behaviors. These behaviors stem from a need to prevent others from judging you harshly for your thoughts and opinions. You may even start to hide who you are to protect yourself. Avoidance is common in emotional, physical, intimate, and sexual relationships because it prevents you from feeling vulnerable. Essentially, it's a protection mechanism. However, it can become dangerous because it can lead to the development of an addiction to people, places, and things to distract you from intimacy in your relationships. You may also start to communicate in an indirect or evasive manner to avoid conflict or confrontation of any kind. It can also create the belief that any display of emotion is a sign of weakness.

Compliance

In order to comply with the wants, needs, and demands of others, you may compromise your own integrity, values, and morals to avoid a person's anger and rejection. This may result from an increased sensitivity to the feelings of other people. It can encourage extreme loyalty in some women, even if their loyalty prevents them from leaving a potentially dangerous situation. Compliance also means that you probably hold other people's feelings, opinions, and thoughts in high esteem. As such, you may find it difficult to express your opinions and feelings, even abandoning your interests for the sake of the other person and their preferences.

Low Self-Esteem

As a woman with codependency, you may find that you have a low self-esteem. This can make it difficult for you to make decisions, cause you to judge yourself harshly, and think that you aren't good enough. When you do receive praise, a compliment, or even a gift, you may feel embarrassed and flustered, perhaps even unworthy of them. Low self-esteem can make it difficult for you to identify your needs or ask for them. Instead, you place a high value on the opinions and thoughts of other people, needing them to approve your behavior, thoughts, feelings, and opinions, which can create "people-pleasing" behavior. People-pleasing is also known as "seeking external validation," which will be covered later in this chapter.

Control Patterns

This pattern stems from a belief that the other person cannot take care of themselves, even if the opposite is true. You may try to manipulate the feelings and thoughts of the other person and then feel resentful when they reject or decline your advice. Control patterns can also take the form of offering unsolicited advice, direction, favors, or gifts to the people that you are trying to influence and control. This pattern may reveal your underlying need to be needed by the other person.

Relationships and Codependency

Healing from your codependency may mean that you need to leave your unhealthy relationship. In this section, I will provide you with a brief overview on how to recover from your codependency if you are in a relationship and don't want to leave. Remember that every relationship is different. This section can be used to help you manage your codependent tendencies, whether you are in a relationship or not.

Take a Break

To successfully heal from codependency, it's recommended by Jones (2020), that you take a break from, or even leave, your relationship so that you have the opportunity, mental energy, and capacity to focus on yourself and the healing process without another person distracting or influencing you. It's important that you resist the urge to start a new relationship as soon as possible because you may fall back into codependent behaviors.

Set Boundaries

Setting boundaries will be discussed in more detail in later chapters; however, it's important to note here that when you start to distance yourself from a codependent relationship, your partner may resist. This could take the form of toxic, manipulative, angry, or even abusive behavior from your ex-partner. It's important that you don't give in. Be consistent and clear with your boundaries so that they will realize that they will have to look for a new relationship from someone else.

Develop and Practice Self-Awareness

When you leave a codependent relationship and start working on healing, you won't be "cured" overnight. It takes time, persistence, and hard work. You will have to actively work on yourself and learn how to ask for and accept help. When you do start a new relationship, you will need to remain alert for any behaviors or signs from your partner that could trigger your codependent behavior. Triggers look different for every woman. They can take the form of sounds, words, the volume of your partner's voice or their behavior. As you start to identify what triggers your codependency, you can create a list of triggers that will help you avoid them in the future, or even prepare you to manage how they impact you.

The Vicious Cycle of Seeking External Validation

Women lose their true identity to codependency. In order to feel validated, they need other people to provide them with validation. A need for external validation often develops as a result of not being able to identify what it is that **you** need and want in life. Looking to external sources for validation is a type of survival mechanism. To successfully recover from codependency, you need to figure out who you are without the rules, expectations, beliefs, and roles determined by other people and the system that you grew up in. Seeking external validation is often an unconscious behavior, but once you start actively noticing it, you can start to make a change.

So what is external validation? It's when a person needs other people to praise them and validate their decisions and worth as a person. They are usually women who did not receive much love and support from their parents, so they look for it somewhere else. External validation is a behavior that is learned from our family systems and environment as children. However, we don't realize that external validation damages our ability to trust ourselves (impacting your self-esteem) because we depend solely on other people's acceptance of us. This may originate from a belief that love is found in your external environment. Your ability to be loved is believed to stem from what you can provide and give to the other person. This is false! You don't need to provide for another person in order to be unconditionally loved and accepted.

A Need for External Validation Originates in Childhood

Seeking external validation is a behavior that normally starts to develop between the ages of six and nine years old (Dee, 2021). You develop this trait as a child because it acts as a survival mechanism that helps you cope in a family system that leaves you feeling emotionally and physically neglected, by your parents or caretakers. When a child is left alone to learn how to love and validate themselves, they will focus on their parents' emotions. This focus stems from the realization that when their parents experienced positive emotions, so could they. It creates a child who focuses on the emotions of others in order to fulfill her own emotional needs.

This also means that you would try to achieve things that would make your parents proud. This is known as "conditional love." It's not healthy because it works on the basis that if you don't act, behave, or look a specific way, then you should feel ashamed. As a child, this led you to associate your identity with specific actions that would elicit feelings of pride and love from your parents toward you. It prevents you from learning how to validate yourself in a healthy way as you grow up, creating an adult who seeks validation from other people, their relationships, and experiences.

Why Is External Validation Bad?

The problem is that human beings are inherently social creatures (Khoghi, 2022). Seeking external validation can actually be healthy and beneficial to a degree. It can help you deal with insecurities about your self-worth and path in life because it feels easier to do something hard when our family system and society approves. We need our social connections to thrive and be happy, but we shouldn't depend on them as our sole source of acceptance and happiness. We need to learn how to provide ourselves with "internal validation." Internal validation is a healthier form of validation seeking because you are in total control. You are the one choosing to validate your decisions and self-worth.

However, you can become addicted to the feeling that being validated by other people brings you without even realizing it. This feeling makes it hard to stop seeking external validation. You continue looking for new ways to receive feelings of love and acceptance so that you can prove to your external environment that you do matter, and you are enough. But you are never satisfied and the feeling of being validated by someone else will eventually wear off. When it does, you start to feel depressed, and your self-confidence drastically declines. You become desperate to feel validated again, so you start doing things that don't make you happy, but may result in someone else validating you.

Stop Relying on External Validation!

In order to stop relying on others to validate you, you need to learn how to rely on yourself. According to Kholghi (2022), the strategies discussed below can help you to stop relying on external validation.

Identify Your Purpose

We all have something in our lives that we are passionate about. This could be a specific topic, hobby, or job. Take a half an hour and ask yourself what is important to you? Define this thing and write it out in detail in your notebook. Don't be ashamed or embarrassed because it doesn't matter if other people support you. Doing or being part of something that matters to you will help you feel fulfilled and increase your self-esteem.

What Is More Fulfilling Than External Validation?

Make sure that the thing that you are choosing is more fulfilling than your need for external validation. This thing could change over months and years. That's normal! We are human beings who are constantly learning and growing. It's okay to allow what we deem our 'purpose' to change as we do. Then, start taking the steps that you need to fulfill your purpose.

Ignore Unsolicited Feedback and Criticism

Everyone always has an opinion and while it's good, even

helpful, to get feedback and advice from a mentor, you need to understand and remember that the advice and opinions given by strangers—or even people that you care about—without asking them won't always be beneficial or helpful. Ignore it! Learn to value your own beliefs about your achievements.

Hard Work Can Silence the Opinions of Others

As you work on fulfilling your purpose (even if it's only a hobby), allow yourself to focus on the process so that there isn't time to listen to peoples' unwanted criticisms.

Keep Your Projects to Yourself Until They Are Complete

It's normal to want to share your new projects with others, especially when it's something that you are particularly passionate about. However, this need often stems from an unconscious need for external validation. Rather, try to wait until your project is over halfway, or finished completely, before sharing it with others. This can create the motivation that you need to encourage yourself to finish your project.

Love Yourself

This topic will be discussed in more detail in chapters 6 and 8. Essentially, self-acceptance can decrease your need for external validation because you are accepting who you are without any conditions. Self-validation and talking back to your inner critic, through the use of affirmations, can help you realize how great you are. Don't be scared to use positive affirmations from the internet to help you. All that matters is that they mean something to you.

Acknowledge and Accept Your Demons

We can't change the past, but we can learn to acknowledge and accept it so that we can move forward with our lives and make a positive change. Self-acceptance is difficult to achieve on your own. Reach out to a therapist if you need help learning how to accept yourself.

Don't Try and Be Better Than Other People

Always trying to be better than the person you deem to be the best will only make you unhappy. You do things that you are uncomfortable with because you are trying to outdo someone else. In reality, the only person that you need to compete with is your past self. Try to be better than she is. You won't always succeed and that's okay. The idea is to use her as a motivation to work toward the independent, healthy woman that you want to be.

Other People Don't Care

This statement is harsh but true. People are often more involved with what is happening in their own lives to really care about what's happening in your life. So live a life that makes you unapologetically happy!

Change Your Social Media Habits

You don't have to delete your social media, but you do need to curate your social media experience so that it encourages positive thoughts instead of feeding negative ones that encourage your codependency and need for external validation. You can practice this by switching off your notifications, changing your profile from 'public' to 'private,' posting things that you like and make you happy, and learning to differentiate between wanting to post something because you actually want to or because you need others to validate you. Remember that your followers don't get to decide your self-worth.

Key Takeaways

- We are all at risk of developing codependency.

- Female gender roles may play an additional risk factor in whether you develop codependency or not.

- Healing from codependency means that you should leave a situation that enables your codependent tendencies and behavior.

- Losing your identity to codependency means that you may look to others to receive validation.

- External validation is used to help women with low self-esteem feel worthy even though they are worthy regardless of whether someone else validates them.

Activity

You can recover from codependency using a variety of activities and exercises that can be practiced at home. However, you may find that you need additional external help and that's okay! Speaking with a licensed mental health practitioner can benefit you and help you on your journey to recovery. Whether you are working with a professional or by yourself, you can use the following exercises to help you work on identifying and combating codependency.

1. In your notebook, reflect on your relationship with yourself, your partner, friends, and family members. Identify any signs of codependency and write them down.

2. You may struggle to take responsibility for your feelings and behavior, but it is important to start taking charge and accepting responsibility because you cannot heal if you don't accept your own role in codependency. Start small.

If your codependency is triggered, remind yourself that you have control over your emotions and behavior. As a result, you are the only person who can make changes to your behaviors and emotions.

3. Find three different positive affirmations on the internet that mean something to you and make you feel good. Write these affirmations on three separate index cards and keep them in your pocket, purse, or bag during the day. Whenever you start to feel any type of negative emotion, read one of these affirmations out loud to yourself.

CHAPTER 4

You Lost Yourself:
Enabling, Fixing, and Controlling
the Men Around You

We are lovable, even if the most important person in your
world rejects you, you are still real, and you are still okay.
–Melody Beattie

Codependency is a behavior that we learn as children from our parents or caregivers. Young girls who grew up in a home with parents who found it difficult to establish and maintain healthy boundaries, were prone to self-sacrificing behavior, had trouble communicating in a healthy way, as well as difficulty saying "no" to others are at a higher risk of growing up to become codependent adults. A lack of good role models makes it difficult for these young girls to grow up into women who have healthy relationships, can establish healthy boundaries, and effectively solve problems in their relationships. As an adult woman who is codependent, you might find yourself prone to entering relationships with people who are codependent or have a problem with addiction. A codependent woman may not believe that she is worthy of being loved and thinks that she should settle for less than she deserves, leading to unhealthy relationships where she may allow emotional, mental, physical, and sexual abuse from her partner.

Relationships and Codependency

In the previous chapters, I discussed how codependency results from our childhood trauma and growing up in a home with caregivers who were unable to teach us how to create healthy relationships, or put ourselves before others. A lack of good role models makes it difficult to grow into a healthy adult woman that can function in the world in a healthy way. Instead, you imitate the behaviors and relationships that you grew up with because you don't know that different, healthier relationships exist. It's easy to enter into a codependent relationship when you never learned how to create and maintain a healthy, two-sided, and mutually beneficial relationship.

There are two types of relationships:

- **Interdependent or healthy relationships:** Both

partners are able to rely on each other and benefit from their relationship. Each person is able to express their emotions in a healthy manner and solve problems without hurting their partner. As such, each partner finds value in their relationship.

- **Codependent or unhealthy relationships:** Partners in an unhealthy relationship normally consist of two codependent partners, or a codependent partner and an individual struggling with an addiction. This is called a codependent relationship. A woman who is codependent finds it difficult to feel as though she has self-worth unless she is needed by someone. Hence, the tendency of a codependent woman to enter a relationship with an individual struggling with an addiction. This relationship is normally one-sided, with only one partner benefiting at the expense of the codependent woman.

Symptoms of a Codependent Relationship

A codependent relationship has similar symptoms to a woman who is codependent. Reflect on your current or past relationships. In your notebook, write down which of the symptoms below you can relate to in the relationship that you reflected on. Determine whether your relationship is (or was) codependent. According to Berry (2017), in a codependent relationship you

- don't experience satisfaction or happiness unless you are doing something for your partner.

- may be aware that your relationship is unhealthy and that your partner's behavior hurts you, but you stay with them.

- do whatever it takes to satisfy and please your partner at your own expense.

- experience constant anxiety about your relationship.

- use all of your time and energy to please your partner.

- feel guilty and ashamed when you think about, or do things, for yourself.

- refrain from expressing your needs and desires.

- ignore your values and morals to meet your partner's expectations, needs, and desires.

Types of Attachment

Our relationships are affected by how we attach ourselves to other people. In a codependent relationship, the nearly obsessive behavior of the codependent partner will affect their relationships and personal needs, as well as their relationship with family, friends, and work colleagues. Your style of attachment is developed from infancy. The type of attachment that you develop is instinctual. This means that you don't actively choose which type of attachment style you are prone to practicing. As a child, your style of attachment formed the foundation on which you learned how to give and receive love and attention as you grew up. Identifying your attachment style will help you understand how your thoughts and behaviors are affected in a relationship. After reading through this section, write down, in detail, the style that you identify with the most in your notebook. There are four main styles of attachment according to MacWilliam (2021).

Anxious Attachment

You have a desire to be in a relationship, but you enter into a relationship where you are not treated right by your partner. Or you enter a relationship where you give yourself completely to your partner so that your relationship will be successful, losing your authentic self in the process.

Avoidant Attachment

Generally, you are suspicious of relationships and intimacy. If you do enter into a relationship, you may have a habit of distancing yourself from your partner. If you feel threatened at any time during your relationship, you may withdraw from it to protect yourself.

Disorganized Attachment

When a woman has a simultaneous desire for, and fear of, relationships and intimacy. You may dissociate, give mixed signals to your partner, or become emotionally overwhelmed whenever you experience pressure or stress in your relationship.

Secure Attachment

One of the healthier forms of attachment. You enjoy your relationship and the closeness it brings you. However, you appreciate your time with and without your partner. You do not experience an overwhelming fear if you need to compromise. There is a lack of negative emotions that make you feel controlled or suffocated by your partner.

How Do Women End up in Codependent Relationships?

It's difficult for you to identify a healthy relationship when you grew up in a dysfunctional home, or a home where you shared a codependent relationship with your parents. This means that you are more likely to unconsciously pursue relationships that were similar to those you grew up with. There are three main factors that contribute to a woman entering into a codependent relationship as an adult, both knowingly and unknowingly. After reading through this section, write down which factors you relate to, or recognize, from your own childhood. Remember that understanding how your codependency developed will help you notice these behaviors in your daily life and relationships. This will help you pursue healthier behavior and relationships in the future.

You Had a Difficult Relationship With Your Parents or Caretakers

When I say "difficult" or "damaging," I'm not specifically referring to abuse, neglect, or a lack of happy memories growing up. You can remember your childhood as happy but still have had a damaging relationship with your parents. As children, our parents are our main role models because we often spend the most time with them. They have a responsibility to teach us how to take care of ourselves and successfully live in an ever changing world. Unfortunately, even when our parents do their best, we can still develop codependency.

As a child, your parents may have unintentionally taught you that if you try to pay attention to your needs or pursue things for yourself, then you are selfish. To cope, you started focusing on your parents' needs instead. Eventually, it was easier to ignore your own needs and cater to what your parents needed so that you wouldn't have to feel negative emotions, like guilt and shame. In such instances, your parents may have been part of one of two groups: They suffered from addiction, or they were not emotionally developed or mature enough at that stage to raise children (which normally occurs when your parents suffered from issues with codependency, addiction, or a lack of emotional maturity), leading to self-centered needs. In both cases, their children would grow up to become codependent adults.

You Lived With a Family Member Who Was Mentally or Physically Ill

Taking care of someone who suffers from chronic or mental illness is a big responsibility, especially if you are a child. Essentially, you took on an adult responsibility before you were ready, without any prior experience that could help you cope under the immense stress, pressure, and responsibility that such a situation would bring. It became easier for you to ignore your own needs and wants so that you could care for your ill family member. This eventually turned into a habit.

You may find that since you were a child, you automatically took on the role of caretaker, no matter what situation you were in. One example of such a role includes what is called the "mom friend" in a friend group. The mom friend takes care of her other friends and focuses on their needs. Your self-worth starts to become dependent on others needing you even though you get nothing in return. This often occurs in cases where your parents, or caretaker, display dysfunctional behaviors that make you feel as though taking on more responsibility than a child your age should is your only choice if you want to survive.

You Grew up in a Home Where Mental, Physical, Emotional, or Sexual Abuse Were Prevalent

Chapter 2 focused on the influence of childhood trauma on codependency. Additionally, trauma also puts you at risk of entering into an abusive relationship as an adult. Growing up in an abusive home, children learn to repress their emotions in order to keep themselves safe. This defense mechanism helps them to cope and survive in a hostile environment. Unfortunately, this means that as a child you learn to care more about other peoples' needs than your own. It becomes a toxic habit that stays with you as you grow up, creating a codependent woman who ignores her own needs and emotions.

I'm not saying that you are guaranteed to enter into an abusive relationship as an adult if you experienced abuse as a child. Many women have been able to break this cycle. I'm trying to inform you that you have a higher risk of entering into an abusive relationship compared to a woman who grew up in a healthy and safe home environment. The physical, spiritual, mental, and emotional impact of abuse can affect you for years after it has ended. Remember that the abuse you experienced is **not** your fault. You need to be aware of the negative impact that abuse has, which can put you at risk of further abuse as an adult. If you are aware of this risk, then you have a greater chance of identifying a potential abusive relationship before entering into it, allowing you to protect yourself from further harm.

Why Do Women Find It Difficult to Leave a Codependent Relationship?

When codependency is all that you know, it makes it difficult to leave. Change is scary and as strange as it may sound, leaving a codependent relationship to pursue a healthier relationship can be terrifying. A codependent relationship's core trait is the dependence of one partner on the other. Dependence on another person makes it difficult for you to be alone. Therefore, it's easier—and feels safer—to remain in a codependent relationship. However, some codependent women may enter into a codependent relationship quickly because when she is single, she feels unwanted, worthless, or rejected. In this case, being single brings up painful emotions that she experienced when she was a child growing up in a codependent or abusive home. There are a variety of reasons why you may find it difficult to leave a codependent relationship. You may even have a number of reasons for staying in a loveless and unhealthy partnership. I will discuss some of these reasons below. Read through this section with an open mind and, if you relate to any of these reasons, note them in your notebook and reflect on why you might feel this way.

You Struggle to Separate Your Identity From Your Partner's Identity

In both situations, you end up staying in an unhealthy and codependent relationship where your life revolves around your partner. Eventually, you can't separate your partner's identity from your own. Your identities become tangled like a pair of headphones that are put into a pocket. It feels near impossible to untangle them, but if you have enough patience, persistence, and you are willing to put in the hard work, you can untangle them. Once you start separating yourself from your partner, you can start recognizing what you really feel about them, what it is that you need in your life, and how you can meet these needs.

Emotions Cloud Your Judgment

I know this idea may seem cliché, but emotions like love, infatuation, and dependency can be intense. As such, it becomes easy for your judgment to be clouded when you experience these emotions. In simple terms, it becomes difficult for you to look at your relationship objectively and make a decision about whether to stay or leave without bias. Additionally, your relationship may reflect the relationships you were exposed to as a child. The codependent relationships that you saw as a child seem normal to you because you don't know that a healthier, mutually beneficial relationship is an option. This isn't anything to be ashamed of! We often only start realizing that the experiences and relationships we grew up with weren't normal or healthy until we are exposed to the world and different relationships. Such exposure is often what triggers our brain to go, "Hey, maybe that experience wasn't normal; maybe I did experience trauma."

Your Relationship Can Be Codependent Even if Your Partner Makes You Happy

It's difficult to determine if your relationship is codependent when you experience moments where you feel safe, loved, and happy. After all, if you are creating happy memories with your partner, then your relationship can't be unhealthy, right? This may be the hardest part of recognizing whether your relationship is codependent or not. Even in an unhealthy relationship, not every moment will be bad. Your partner might promise you that they are going to change their behavior for the better. They may even follow through on those promises...at least for a while. Then things start getting bad again. It becomes a never ending cycle of good moments, not good or bad moments, and then bad moments that make it hard to determine if your relationship is codependent or not.

A Codependent Partner

Your partner might be codependent. This means that they will struggle to end the relationship and let you go. They may try to manipulate you by pursuing you even after your relationship has ended, refuse to take "no" as an answer, or their behavior might make you feel uncomfortable and unsafe. In a severe case, you may need to involve the relevant authorities. However, in most scenarios, as long as you remain firm, uphold your boundaries, and refrain from pursuing the relationship again, then your ex-partner should come to the realization that they will need to find someone else.

Self-Sacrificing Behavior Is Socially Acceptable

Have you ever noticed how women who focus on themselves and put themselves first are called selfish, greedy, or uncaring? That is because self-sacrificing behavior is socially acceptable, especially if you are a woman. From the moment you are born up till your death, society—and even friends, family, and partners—may encourage you to take on the role of caretaker or giver and put your own needs aside. It's a dangerous and destructive behavior that can severely impact you, leaving you burnt out, emotionally drained, or stuck in a dangerous situation. The perceived normality of self-sacrificing behavior makes it difficult for many women to feel comfortable taking time to themselves without feeling guilty or ashamed. But this doesn't mean that self-care or putting yourself first is bad. In fact, it's the complete opposite. I will elaborate in detail the benefits of self-care in Chapter 6.

Guilt and Shame

Guilt and shame are big factors that prevent women from leaving codependent relationships. These two emotions often play a large role in codependent behaviors and relationships. Shame generally stems from a belief that you are worthless if you are not needed by others, or able to give them something. This belief is toxic and untrue, but realizing and acknowledging that doesn't mean that these feelings magically disappear. They keep you isolated, and if you do try to leave a codependent relationship, others may tell you that you should stay because your partner needs you. These people disregard the fact that you are being negatively impacted by this relationship and may shame you instead of helping you. Remember that not everyone will do this, but even the idea that someone may behave this way might prevent you from seeking help to leave a codependent relationship.

How to Cope With Leaving a Codependent Relationship

Ask for help! Speak with a trusted family member, friend, or seek the guidance of a qualified mental health practitioner to help you successfully leave your codependent relationship. Recovering from a codependent relationship requires you to heal from your codependent tendencies. You can use the various strategies discussed throughout this book to help you create your own plan to leave your codependent partner and avoid codependent relationships in the future. Additionally, you can use Martin's (2021) suggestions on how to end a codependent relationship.

- Take notice of and acknowledge the factors that make it difficult to change your codependent thoughts and behaviors.

- Create a codependency recovery plan that attends to each area of your life where codependency has impacted you.

- Learn how to validate and love yourself and recognize your needs and emotions.

- Start pursuing your own goals and interests despite the guilt that you may feel.

- Practice self-care.

- Learn how to effectively manage your anxiety, solve conflict in a healthy manner, and how to be more assertive in your life.

- Learn about healthy relationships, what they look like, and what you should look for before entering into a relationship.

- Start challenging the voice in your head that says that you have to save, heal, and help others without any regard for your health or safety.

- Use affirmations to help you combat your negative thinking about your self-worth.

Why Codependent Women Have a Tendency to Enter Relationships With Addicts

A relationship between a codependent woman and a person who suffers from an addiction problem may sound like a good combination, especially when you consider the fact that her codependency means that she would like to help her partner. In reality, such a relationship can be even more dangerous than a codependent relationship. A woman who is codependent often looks to her external environment for things that will make her feel worthy and loved. When she meets a person who suffers from an addiction problem, she may see no problem with pursuing a relationship with them because she believes she can 'help' them.

In this type of relationship, you (as the codependent) may unconsciously protect your partner from the consequences of their addiction. This can take the form of taking on responsibility for your partner's finances, relationships with other people, and obligations as an adult. For example, you might pay off the debt that your partner created due to their addiction, or you may find yourself making excuses for them and their behavior. Eventually, the partner who struggles with addiction has a large amount of free time because their codependent partner has taken control of everything else, allowing their struggle with addiction to become worse. The codependent partner really is only trying to help her partner, but soon she may also start spiraling out of control. This can create feelings of resentment and anger from both partners. She may not even realize that she is unintentionally enabling her partner's addiction for fear of what may happen should they recover.

Examples of a Codependent Relationship With a Partner Who Struggles With Addiction

According to Utti (2016), a codependent relationship where one partner has issues with addiction can take the form of a wife who justifies her husbands drinking by saying that he had a difficult day at work and needs to relax, a parent who takes on extra responsibility in the home because her partner has been drinking or taking drugs, or a woman who excuses her partner's absence from an event by lying; when in reality, her partner is at home, under the influence of heroin.

When a codependent woman enters into a relationship with an

addict, her reasons for staying include her subconscious hope that her partner will change. She believes that if she stays, her partner will see what she is able to provide them with love, understanding, and support. Additionally, she might believe that once her partner sees what she can offer them, they will give her the love and validation that she desires. In reality, she ends up staying in an unhealthy relationship that negatively impacts both of them. However, if you never learned what a healthy relationship looked like, then how are you supposed to create one?

Behaviors of a Codependent Woman in a Relationship With a Person Struggling With Addiction

There are a number of common behaviors that a codependent woman takes part in when she is in a relationship with a person who struggles with addiction. According to Gate House (2020), if you are a codependent woman that is in a relationship with someone who struggles with addiction, you may notice that you take part in some, or perhaps all, of the behaviors discussed below.

Take Responsibility for Her Partner

As a codependent woman, you already feel some degree of responsibility for your partner's thoughts, feelings, and decisions. If your partner struggles with addiction, you may try to help them by solving their addiction problem and giving them advice that they never asked for. You may even resort to manipulative behavior to try and retain control of your relationship and encourage your partner to continue relying on you. Unfortunately, you can also start feeling resentful and angry toward your partner.

You Put Your Partner's Needs Before Your Own

Codependent women often lose their identities to their relationships. This can result in feelings of shame, guilt, worthlessness, and a lack of self-esteem. Losing your identity while also attending to your partner's needs can overwhelm you. You might make unhealthy decisions that make you uncomfortable so that you can prove your loyalty and worth to your partner. As such, you struggle to set and maintain healthy boundaries, doubting your perception of your relationship.

You Fear Being Alone

A fear of being alone is common amongst many codependent women. Especially as being codependent already means that you fear being abandoned or rejected by the people that you care about. Your desire and need for acceptance and approval, which originate from your childhood, drive you to pursue and stay in a codependent relationship. However, you may start feeling resentful toward your partner's problem with addiction.

Your fear of being alone prevents you from leaving your position as their caretaker, even when your attempts to please your partner make you uncomfortable and unhappy.

An Inability to Recognize and Express Your Emotions in Your Relationship

Codependent women have a tendency to ignore their needs and emotions. This makes it difficult for you to separate who you really are from who you perceive yourself to be. You may be prone to imitating your partner's emotions instead of experiencing your own. It's easy to understand that you should leave your codependent relationship to ensure your own well-being, but it's difficult to put it into practice because you don't want to upset your partner. A persistent focus on the needs and emotions of your partner may manifest as severe anxiety that makes it even more difficult for you to ask for help.

Key Takeaways

- Codependency is learned from childhood, especially from our parents or caretakers.

- A lack of exposure to healthy relationships as you grew up makes it difficult to build and maintain your own healthy relationship.

- The symptoms of a codependent relationship are similar to the symptoms of codependency.

- Your style of attachment will affect your thoughts and behaviors in a relationship.

- In a codependent relationship, it's easy to lose your identity. It becomes difficult to know who you are without your partner.

- Codependent women are prone to entering relationships with a person who has issues with addiction because of her tendency to look to her external environment for feelings of validation, worth, love, and happiness.

Practical Exercises

For this activity, you will need your notebook and colored pencils. Find a quiet place that is comfortable and allows you to focus. Then, turn to a blank page in your notebook. Please read through this activity before practicing it so that you know what to expect. This activity, according to MacWilliams (2021), will help you improve your ability to connect to yourself in a healthy way by becoming aware of what's happening inside your mind and body.

1. Start by taking a deep breath in, then slowly breathe out. As you breathe, notice how your stomach, lungs, ribs, and chest expand and contract, creating a space inside of your body to store the air. Pay attention to how this space becomes bigger with each breath. Now, start focusing on your thoughts.

2. Do you notice a specific question, stressor, or anxiety appearing? This can be anything that makes you feel restless.

3. Now take that inquiry and imagine that you are dropping it from your mind into your body. Where does this inquiry land? Using a colored pencil (the color should represent your specific inquiry), express the color on a clear page in your notebook. It can be a specific shape or have no form at all, do what feels right.

4. Assign a shape that feels right to your drawing. You can assign this shape in step 3 or after you have completed step three.

5. Reflect on your inquiry. Imagine associating a line with it. What does this line look like? Is it straight, curved, or jagged? Using a new color (that represents the line), add this line to your drawing.

6. Observe your drawing. Notice how much space it does

and does not take up on the page. Then, think about where your drawing is in comparison to your body. When you look at your drawing, does it feel as though it's found on your torso, or perhaps it represents your head? Whichever body part it represents, add your missing body parts to the drawing.

7. Ask yourself what sound your drawing would make if it could make a sound. You can listen to this sound or write down the sound that you associate with your drawing.

8. Imagine your drawing in relation to your body again and think about what movement it would make. What would this movement look like and how does it make you want to move when you look at your drawing?

9. Once you have completed the above steps, assign a feeling to each step of this activity. This word should be descriptive because it aims to help you connect to your true feelings.

10. Repeat this activity whenever you feel like getting in touch with your thoughts and emotions, especially during stressful times.

CHAPTER 5

Removing the Victim

*Burn the victim card down to the ground—for you are so much
more than that!*
–Sijdah Hussain

The main goal of codependency recovery is to become a woman
who knows who she is as an individual that values and trusts
herself, is able to express how she feels, and manages her
emotions in a healthy way. Remember that how you see and
value yourself impacts your feelings, thoughts, and how you
behave in your life and relationships. You need to understand
that codependency recovery is possible, but it is a long-term
journey that can be challenging. It requires you to constantly
change and alter the methods that you use to suit where you
currently are in life. Before developing into codependency, you
really are trying to be selfless and caring. You aim to help those
that you care about.

Unfortunately, past experiences warp your selfless behavior, creating a compulsive, codependent relationship between you and another person. This makes it difficult to take the time to care for yourself. If you do try to take time to practice simple self-care, you probably feel guilty and do something for your partner so that you can get rid of this uncomfortable feeling. However, you start to resent your partner when you don't give yourself the same level of care that you give them.

The Victim Mentality in Codependency

Resentment is a common feeling among codependent women. It's understandable. You have gone out of your way to care for, help, and provide for the other person without receiving a simple "thank you" in return. Resentment has become a common feeling. You are aware that you're overworking yourself for someone who does not appear to care. While you may continue to care and provide for your partner, or the other person, you may also start blaming them and feel angry about the situation that you are in without doing anything to change it. This could stem from your need for external validation and an inability to provide yourself with the praise and validation that you deserve.

As a woman who is codependent, you may feel like you are the victim. It's understandable, and to some degree, a true statement. However, this belief that you are a victim can start to take over how you see yourself and your life. It can negatively impact you and start creating additional problems that may cause your codependency to become worse. Using this chapter, in conjunction with Chapter 3, you need to start looking at yourself and start coming to terms with the fact that you may have made yourself the victim.

Please note: While you may have codependency, it doesn't automatically mean that you have a victim mentality. I am not writing this chapter to blame you or point fingers. I am discussing this topic because victim mentality is common among those who have codependency and, in order to effectively recover, you need to understand what it is, how it manifests and affects you, and how you can recover from it.

After experiencing trauma in your childhood, surviving an unhealthy relationship, and recognizing your codependent tendencies, you need to acknowledge that you have experienced negative treatment and pain that you didn't deserve. Acknowledging that you are a victim of unfair treatment during your childhood, and part of your adulthood, is important for cultivating compassion for yourself, forgiving yourself for developing unhealthy coping mechanisms that helped you survive, and starting your recovery process. This acknowledgement that you have been a victim does not mean that your friends, family, or partner are doing things specifically to annoy you or punish you. If you notice that your thoughts start to take on a theme of feeling sorry for yourself, but you don't do anything about it, while continuing to play the victim, then you have started to develop a victim mentality.

What is Victim Mentality?

Victim mentality is a common characteristic of codependency that often occurs on a subconscious level. This means that many women don't even realize that they think this way. However, just because you don't actively realize that you think this way doesn't mean that you won't notice its impact on your life. According to Merriam-Webster (n.d.-b), "victim mentality" is when a woman believes that she is the victim, no matter what situation she is in. It also includes the belief that bad things will always happen to her specifically. As a result, she moves through her life behaving like she is the victim, regardless of whether she is actually a victim or not. She blames other people for her unhappiness and problems, never taking responsibility or making a change. This may result in negative feelings like denial, resentment, pessimism, and sadness.

For example, a codependent woman with a victim mentality may believe that her partner always leaves the dishes in the sink for her to wash. In reality, her partner had an early meeting that morning, followed by a full schedule, which prevented them from doing the dishes before their codependent partner came home.

How Does Victim Mentality Manifest?

The feeling that results from the victim mentality can be difficult to deal with. If a person has addictive tendencies, they may turn to drugs or alcohol to cope by using these substances to numb their feelings. For a codependent woman, this often results in her thoughts becoming more negative, and her codependent tendencies becoming worse. She believes that she doesn't deserve a healthy relationship so why should she try to leave her current relationship? Others may not even realize that she is struggling with this way of thinking. She may appear and act normal on the outside, but on the inside, she is struggling with feelings of depression, unworthiness, weakness, and she may feel powerless to do anything about them. These negative feelings can become worse when you have low self-esteem (another common symptom of codependency). You don't believe that you deserve good things and if you are gifted something that makes you feel good, or improves your life, you might start feeling intense guilt. Your guilt only feeds your negative mindset, and you may spiral, feel depressed, or even develop a mental illness from your struggle to cope with the stress and negativity that this mentality has brought you.

Recovering From Victim Mentality

This way of thinking is unhealthy and dangerous! If you don't try to heal from the victim mentality, it's only going to get worse and you do deserve better, no matter what you think. You may feel as though you don't have the power to make a change, but you do! You have to actively decide to make it, even if you don't currently believe that you can. If you make the decision to change, remain firm in your decision, and work hard even when you experience setbacks, then you will be successful. But it won't happen overnight. Recovery includes noticing and changing how you think, which isn't easy. It's like breaking a bad habit, and if you have any experience with that, then you know that it takes time, patience and persistence.

According to Dominica (2022), your first step to healing from a victim mentality is to acknowledge and recognize that you have a victim mentality. You can use the mindfulness activity at the end of this chapter to help you notice your thoughts. The recovery process is similar to the recovery process of codependency in that sense. Once you overcome your denial (even if it's not perfect), then you can start making a positive change in your life. Then, you need to start seeing yourself as valuable—even if no one else does. You can work on this using the affirmation activity at the end of this chapter. By combining both activities, you will be able to start looking inside of yourself and take notice of who you are as an individual. This is important because it will help you to find your authentic self and start nurturing her. It will help you recognize your good qualities and appreciate them, despite your past actions and behaviors that made you feel bad about yourself.

Recovering from the victim mentality means that you stand up for yourself and believe that you are no longer a victim, remaining firm in this decision. Cognitive behavioral therapy, mindfulness exercises, and affirmations are useful tools for recovering from a victim mentality. While these tools will be discussed throughout this chapter, you have to learn how to take responsibility for your thoughts, behaviors, and actions first.

Start Taking Responsibility for Your Life

I won't disagree with the fact that there are occasions where you are a victim due to the actions of others or unforeseen circumstances. However, you have to learn how to take responsibility in order to stop seeing yourself as a victim. A general trait among codependents is that it's extremely difficult to take responsibility when something bad happens, but quite easy when something good happens. You may be used to blaming others when something bad or inconvenient happens to you so that you can avoid dealing with your uncomfortable feelings, as well as the consequences that may arise by taking responsibility in that situation. But taking responsibility can mean that you are accepting that you may be at fault for something, or that there are certain actions that you could be taking in a certain situation but aren't.

It's important for you to note that you have the ability to choose whether you will see a situation as positive or negative. You can choose how you will respond. It's true that you aren't always responsible for something happening, but you are responsible for reacting in a way that aligns with your values, beliefs, and goals in life. You can use the following strategies to help you learn how to feel comfortable taking responsibility.

Actively Decide How You Want to Spend Your Time

I'm sure you have heard someone say that they just don't have enough time to do what they want in a single day. You may have even used this sentence yourself. You need to perceive time not as a powerful entity that controls you, but as a valuable resource that will help you during your day. Time doesn't have control over you. The way that you create and organize your priorities is what steals time from you. Decide to take responsibility and reflect on how you prioritize things in your life. Identify what is actually important to you and create a detailed list of your priorities. Now, use your time to attend to this list. If you feel that you are wasting your time on one of these activities, then you need to remove it from your list and reprioritize it. This takes a lot of trial and error, but it will help you take responsibility for your time and figure out what is important to you.

You Have the Power to Control Your Life

In simple terms, don't blame others when something goes wrong. The situation that you are currently in is a result of your actions and behavior (please note that this **does not** apply to abusive, dangerous, or harmful situations). Recognizing that you have control over a situation can help you understand that it's possible to change your life, make healthy choices, and implement your decisions without allowing another person to influence or control you.

Be Aware of the Future and Prepare for It

Proactivity is a tool that you can use to implement change when you are unhappy about a situation. It helps you feel comfortable taking control of your life. Although, it's important that you don't overwhelm yourself by trying to do everything at once. Take small steps that are easy to implement and manage. Remember that change is scary! But smaller steps will help you adjust and react to obstacles in a healthy way without being setback.

Learn to Love Yourself

Using tools such as mindfulness and affirmations, you can learn how to love yourself without judgment. Self-love is an important practice because it helps you live a healthy life where you value yourself and don't allow others to impact your self-esteem in a negative way. You learn how to praise and validate yourself without relying on others. This can help you live a happy and independent life.

Cognitive Behavioral Therapy as a Codependency Recovery Method

Cognitive Behavioral Therapy (CBT) is a codependency recovery tool that often requires the assistance of a qualified therapist. In this section, I will provide you with a brief overview of CBT so that you can decide if it's a treatment that you would like to consider pursuing.

What Is Cognitive Behavioral Therapy?

Women who are codependent are often focused on their external environment. This makes it difficult for you to identify what is happening in your mind. If you have codependency and focus on your external environment, you may believe that because you feel helpless in a situation you are a victim. This develops into the victim mentality, which I discussed earlier in this chapter. CBT is a tool that is used by therapists to help you change your unhelpful way of thinking and notice the behavior patterns that reinforce these thoughts. You then learn how you can change them so that you can develop healthy behaviors that reinforce positive thoughts that don't promote a victim mentality. During this therapy, your therapist aims to provide you with guidance and support so that you can find out who you are without codependency.

The Impact of Cognitive Behavioral Therapy

Remember that codependency reinforces negative feelings such as pain, anger, and resentment (toward yourself and others) that create problems in your thought process and impact your ability to effectively solve problems. CBT teaches you how to take notice of your thoughts and beliefs, acknowledge them, and then identify a healthier way of viewing a situation that is closer to reality. This technique involves the use of mindfulness.

Mindfulness in CBT is used to teach you that you always have a choice in how you can react in a situation. It helps you realize that other people don't control you. You are responsible for the changes that you want to make in your life. Yes, you may need help from other people, or tools such as CBT, but it's up to you to make the decision to make a change. This decision can help you realize that your codependent behavior is how your mind has chosen to respond to the trauma that you have suffered. You don't have to be a victim for the rest of your life. CBT helps you understand that it's possible to be compassionate toward yourself and work toward a healthier life.

Key Takeaways

- The main goal of codependency recovery is to become a healthy, independent woman who is in control of her life.

- Victim mentality develops when a codependent woman starts to believe that she is a victim no matter the circumstances.

- Women often struggle with this type of thinking without other people ever noticing.

- CBT, mindfulness meditation, positive affirmations, and taking responsibility for yourself are codependency recovery methods.

Activities

Mindfulness Activity

Mindfulness is a tool that you can use to notice *where* your attention is, and take control of it, without judging yourself. As a codependent woman, you probably struggle with negative thoughts and focusing because your attention is concentrated on other people and never on yourself. Through this activity, you will learn to pay attention to your mind and body—without judging yourself—so that you can notice your negative thoughts without getting attached to them. It will help you separate your thoughts from yourself so that their power over you and your emotions can be removed. This is a five-minute exercise that you can use to regulate your emotions whenever you feel stressed or anxious.

1. Start by finding a comfortable place in your home to sit, stand, or lie down.

2. Set your phone's timer for five minutes.

3. Close your eyes and pay attention to how you are breathing.

4. Slowly move your focus from your breathing to your thoughts.

5. Simply notice your thoughts as they pass you by. Don't focus on them.

6. If you struggle to let your thoughts pass you by, start paying attention to your breath and repeat the exercise until your timer rings.

Affirmation Activity

Affirmations are a useful tool for changing negative thoughts to ones that are more positive. As a codependent woman, creating and accepting positive statements about yourself is difficult. However, if you are persistent, you will be able to change your attitude and beliefs, develop a love for yourself, and improve your self-esteem. There are a variety of affirmations available on the internet. If you use the following key terms and phrases, you will be able to find an abundance of affirmations on the internet.

- affirmations

- affirmations for self-love

- affirmations for codependency

- affirmations for codependent women

According to Kristenson (2022), the following list is an example of the types of affirmations available:

- I am not responsible for the emotions of others.

- It's okay to put myself first.

- It's not my job to fix others.

- I am a good person.

- I won't punish myself anymore

For this exercise, create a list of 5-10 positive affirmations that mean something to you. You can use the list above or find your own affirmations using the key terms above.

1. Once you have created this list, alter the affirmations to suit your life and circumstances as everyone experiences codependency differently.

2. Copy them into your notebook and onto index cards. You should write one affirmation per index card.

3. Repeat these affirmations out loud to yourself, every morning after you wake up and before you go to bed, as well as several times during the day. Repeating these affirmations is especially important when you are angry, sad, stressed, or feeling resentful toward others or even yourself. If you are consistent in your practice, your brain will start to believe what you are repeating to yourself. This will help you to develop a more positive outlook where you are not the victim.

CHAPTER 6

The Basics of Self-Care

It's about progress, not perfection.
–Sharon Martin

Codependent women often feel overwhelmed and underappreciated. Prioritizing the needs of others is normal in codependency and contributes to these negative feelings that create resentment toward the people that you care about. When you are codependent, you sacrifice yourself so that you can give others what they need, but what about what you need?

The Importance of Self-Care in Codependency

When you think about the term "self-care," your mind probably remembers ads with famous actresses who somehow look glamorous in their pajamas as they sit on their couch, trying to convince you to buy a beauty product—like a cream, soap, or perfume—to "treat yourself." This is what the media portrays as self-care, but that's not what it looks like in reality. Codependency uses all of your physical and emotional energy to care for your partner while leaving nothing for you. This state is known as burn out. Self-care is about using your energy to take the time to provide yourself with the same love and care that you give everyone else so that you can feel rested, recharged, loved, valued, and worthy. It is essential to your recovery journey.

It's difficult to start practicing self-care when you are codependent because all your life you have believed that any care that you give yourself means that you are selfish. This belief is toxic and can harm you. You may give up on self-care to avoid the feelings of guilt that arise when you begin taking care of yourself. These uncomfortable feelings are responsible for preventing many women from starting—or continuing—to take care of themselves. Self-care is difficult to start practicing as a codependent woman because you are breaking the habit of not taking care of yourself. It will feel easier to give up self-care the minute you start feeling guilty and uncomfortable. While it may be easier to give up, it will only hurt you. No one else is going to take care of you. You have to decide for yourself whether you will continue to stick with your decision, even when you encounter obstacles.

Self-care teaches you how to trust yourself so that you can meet your needs, discover the woman you really are, and learn what makes you happy. You will learn how to stop judging yourself and be compassionate to the woman that you have become instead. It teaches you how to meet your needs, pursue your goals, and live your authentic life without feeling guilty about it. You learn that your self-worth is not dependent on others because you are the only one who gets to decide your worth. Codependency makes it hard enough to take proper care of yourself, so start small! Self-care is about progress. It's better to take small steps that help you to improve your life and meet your needs than going big and stopping your self-care routine because it started to overwhelm you.

Practicing Self-Care

Effectively practicing self-care means that you need to know what *your* mind and body need because it looks different for everyone. In this section, I will provide you with some basic self-care strategies that are commonly used, as well as tips to help you get started, so that you can tailor your self-care routine to your needs and lifestyle. When you practice self-care, you have to pay attention to what your mind and body need so that you can provide these needs without draining your energy. This practice is meant to make you happy, feel loved, and inspired to carry on with your day. If your self-care doesn't elicit such feelings, then you need to change the strategies that you are using. Self-care doesn't need you to learn new skills or buy fancy tools, you only need to give yourself permission to provide yourself with the loving care that you have been denied for so long.

As a codependent woman, you may struggle with starting a self-care routine because of the guilty feelings it elicits. The best way to work around this is to care for yourself like a child because you also need to eat, sleep, and shower. Basic needs that, when properly met, can make a big difference in how you feel during the day, both mentally and physically. Using the following questions as your starting point, I want you to create your own list of basic needs in your notebook. As you start answering these questions, you can add personal notes that will help you better meet this need in the future.

- Have I eaten a proper meal today?

- Did I drink water today?

- How much sleep did I get? If your answer is below seven hours, consider taking a nap.

- Is my daily schedule predictable? A predictable schedule

can reduce any unpredictability that makes you feel anxious about waking up for the day or starting tasks.

- How do my friends and family treat me? Remember that if your relationships are unhealthy, they will impact how you treat yourself.

- Have you taken part in any fun and stimulating activities today? Taking part in a hobby or outside activity, like gardening, can provide your brain with healthy stimuli that fuels creativity and prevents boredom.

- Have you gone outside today? Consider combining this point with the above and go for a short walk in a park, or around the block, once a day.

- Did you take some time to play today? Look, I know you're an adult, but play is something that we all need. It can re-energize you, fuel creativity, help you destress, and find something to look forward to each day. You could take part in a sport, play with your dog or cat, or take some time to work on a hobby. Don't be afraid to try new things. It's the only way you'll be able to determine what makes you happy. You may feel a bit ridiculous, but remember that other people are too involved in their own lives to care about what you are doing in yours, so you may as well enjoy yourself.

- How can you soothe yourself when you feel stressed or anxious? Soothing behaviors can take the form of stimming behaviors—like playing with a fidget toy, enjoying a hot drink, or talking to yourself in the mirror as you repeat positive affirmations. You will need to try out various soothing behaviors to see what works best for you.

Self-Care Strategies

Once you have created your list of basic needs, you can now look at some of the strategies that form the foundation of a good self-care routine. You don't have to do it perfectly. Self-care is about providing yourself with the love and care that you have been lacking in your life. You may have days where you struggle and that's okay. We all have days like that. This is where your self-care routine comes in. If you find that you don't have the energy to take part in complicated self-care activities, start small, and refer back to this list. Take the time to recover and be compassionate toward yourself when you are struggling.

Check-In

Codependent women struggle to be constantly aware of what is happening in their mind and body in the present moment. When you start practicing self-care, you need to learn how to tell yourself the truth so that you can meet your needs, remove yourself from an overwhelming or uncomfortable situation, or take note of your feelings. To do this, you have to create an awareness of what's happening in your body by checking-in. Throughout your day, take a moment to ask yourself the following questions:

- What am I feeling at this moment? Describe how you feel mentally and emotionally. Are you tired, stressed, or overwhelmed?

- How am I physically feeling? Take note of how your body feels. Are you tense, do you have any pain, are you hungry?

- Where are my thoughts? This question helps you take note of whether your mind is in the present moment, focused on the past, or stressing about the future.

After answering these questions, you will have a starting point that will help you create a customized self-care routine. This will help you to meet your needs in the present moment without overwhelming yourself or stressing about things that are out of your control. Use the list in the previous section to help you meet the needs that these questions have identified.

Be Consistent

You can't practice self-care once a month and expect to see a difference. This is an everyday practice that requires you to remain persistent, even on your bad days. It will be hard at first, especially when you start out. Don't berate yourself for this. It takes time to build a new habit, especially because taking care of yourself is not something that you will be used to doing. Start small and break your self-care into manageable steps that you are comfortable with. The best way to develop consistency is to create a daily schedule that you can refer to when your codependency is triggered. A visual aid that has dedicated self-care slots can make it easier to remain consistent when you start practicing self-care because it's like attending to the items on a to-do list.

Be Kind to Yourself!

The journey to recovering is a long one and there may be unforeseen circumstances that trigger your codependent behavior or prevent you from practicing self-care. Life happens and that's okay, but I also know that it isn't that simple. On such occasions, your thoughts may start becoming negative. First, you need to forgive yourself and be compassionate because you are doing your best. Then, you need to challenge these thoughts by using positive affirmations. Affirmations can help you guide your thinking to become more positive. Use affirmations that help you realize that you are worth the time and the effort that you have put in. Your progress doesn't disappear because you happened to have a bad day. Use your positive affirmations from the previous chapter to help you remember what an amazing woman you are.

Let Go

One of the hardest, but perhaps the most important, parts of self-care is learning how to let go of people, situations, and behaviors that enable your codependent behavior. Detaching yourself from the people that you care about can help you to heal from your codependency and encourages others to start taking responsibility for their behavior and actions. This can be hard, especially because you care about them, but if your current relationship is hurting you, then it's not worth your time and energy. Learning to let go means setting healthy boundaries and remaining firm—even when loved ones don't respect them—figuring out who you are as an independent woman, and allowing yourself to pursue a life that makes you happy.

Setting Healthy Boundaries

The theory behind setting healthy boundaries is quite simple. The difficult part is implementing it because those who benefitted from your lack of boundaries may be upset that they can no longer benefit or take advantage of you. You will need to learn to accept that setting boundaries may make those that you care about angry, but the benefits will outlast the few minutes of anger from them. So don't give in!

Setting a boundary is when you create limits on what your partner, friend, boss, or family member can expect from you and your relationship with them. You establish exactly what you are and are not willing to accept in this relationship. This doesn't mean that you can't listen to your partner's problems. It simply means that you won't allow their problems to become yours. Struggling to set and uphold your boundaries benefits your partner as you take on their problems. This can result in codependency.

However, if you and your partner respect each other's boundaries, then you have healthy boundaries. Even if you can't always do what your partner asks of you because of your boundaries, your partner will still love and support you in your relationship, just like you will still love and support them if they don't do something because of their boundaries. So how do you set healthy boundaries?

Identify What You Are and Aren't Comfortable With

You may struggle with creating your boundaries at first because you don't actually know what you are comfortable with after years of doing things for others despite being uncomfortable. Start by creating a written list of what you do and don't feel comfortable with. Ensure that you can edit this list because it will change as you recover from codependency and develop your sense of self-worth.

1. Reflect on past situations where someone asked something of you.

2. Did you say "yes" because you actually wanted to do it, or did you really mean "no"?

3. Did you mean "yes" but change your mind when you started to feel uncomfortable halfway through the activity?

4. Repeat questions 1-3 for each past scenario. This will help you create some basic boundaries where you know what you are and are not comfortable doing. You can also apply these questions to current and future scenarios.

Say "No"

This is difficult when you are codependent, especially when you already have a habit of saying "yes" even when you mean "no." You don't need to feel guilty about this because it's in the past. From this moment, you need to start moving forward to live a healthier life where you mean what you say. Only say "yes" if you do want to do something. Otherwise, embrace saying "no." Start small by saying "no" to little things. Then, imagine scenarios where you firmly say no to someone who asks you to do something you don't want to do. Saying "no" may elicit feelings of guilt. When you start feeling guilty, ask yourself the following questions:

- Do I really want to do what I am being asked?

- Am I comfortable doing it?

- Do I have time?

- Will doing this thing benefit me?

If you answer "no" for each of these questions, then you don't need to feel guilty. Please remember that even if you have the time, it doesn't mean that you should be doing it. There may be times where you can't outright say "no." Instead, you can say "no" without actually saying it. Maybe your partner asks you to do some errands for them and help them with a project for work. In reality, you know that you will have to do all the work, while they get the credit and benefits. However, you can't say "no" either because they will try to guilt trip you. Instead, you could tell them, "Unfortunately, I'm not able to do that." Essentially, you say "no" without saying it directly.

Set Limits

Once you have a basic set of boundaries and you start feeling comfortable saying "no," practice reinforcing your boundaries. Reinforcing your boundaries involves remaining consistent. Don't make exceptions for anyone. Be firm, even when you feel guilty, because you are the one who has to deal with the consequences of your boundaries being broken. Reinforcement is about consistency, remaining firm, and declining requests even when you are scared or feel guilty. You are more capable than you give yourself credit for.

Therapy as a Treatment for Codependency

Recovering from codependency is difficult, I won't lie. It takes a lot of hard work, and you may find it difficult to remain consistent when you are working on your recovery by yourself. It's okay to ask for help. In fact, reaching out can be quite beneficial. Besides CBT, which I discussed in the previous chapter, you can pursue any of the therapies below to help you on your journey to recovery.

Group Therapy

There are many women who struggle with codependency. You aren't alone. Being a part of a codependency recovery group can help you learn how to form a healthy relationship, set boundaries, and get positive feedback on your progress. A group setting will also help you develop your self-esteem, self-awareness, and an awareness of how you feel in the current moment.

Cognitive Therapy

This therapy is similar to CBT. With the help of a qualified therapist, you learn to identify the thoughts that contribute to your codependency, how to tolerate uncomfortable feelings, as well as how you can feel comfortable accepting responsibility for your life.

Family Therapy

This therapy is appropriate if your family struggles with codependency, unhealthy familial relationships, or it has a dysfunctional dynamic. Each member of the family learns skills such as identifying codependent behaviors and patterns, how to create a healthier relationship, and how to effectively communicate.

Tips for Practicing Self-Care

Introducing self-care into your daily routine can be difficult, but don't give up. You can use the tips below to help you implement self-care in your daily life.

Give Yourself Approval

Codependent women seek approval from their external environment. As a codependent woman, you have to learn how to acknowledge the reality of your current situation and accept it. It's hard, but it will help you understand that even though you wish your current situation were different, you are still worthy of love and appreciation, even if you are the one providing it to yourself.

Practice Effective Communication

When you are talking to someone, be clear and direct. Don't try to create hidden meanings or avoid answering a question because you are afraid you will hurt the other person's feelings. They will appreciate honest and direct communication more than words that have a hidden meaning. When you talk to someone, start using 'I' statements. These are sentences that help you express your feelings to the other person when they make you feel uncomfortable, unappreciated, or hurt your feelings (even if they did so unintentionally).

This technique is a great way to improve your relationships because you and your partner know exactly what to expect from each other. You know that they mean exactly what they are saying without any hidden meanings that can be misinterpreted or create future problems. This type of statement is a way to bring attention to how you feel without blaming the other person, preventing animosity from them and opening up an opportunity for honest communication. An example of an "I" statement includes: "I was hurt when you said that you don't like how I dress in front of my family today."

Learn to Accept Uncertainty

You may find that you become attached to a specific outcome. When a situation doesn't happen exactly as you hoped, you start feeling overwhelmed, anxious, and stressed. To practice effective self-care, you need to accept that things don't always turn out how we want them to and that's okay. It's okay to disappoint other people. They may be upset for a few hours, but it won't ruin your relationship. Your worth and value as a person do not depend on the opinions of others and once you realize and accept that, you will feel free to pursue the life that you want to live.

Allow Yourself to Be Selfish

Give yourself permission to be happy and take the time to care for yourself. To prevent resentment toward others, anger, or feelings of being overwhelmed, you need to learn to take time for yourself to do what you want to do, even if that means you aren't doing anything. It's okay to be selfish. You have needs and wants that deserve attention. You don't have to prove yourself or your worth in order to meet them.

Learn to Value Yourself

Don't rely on others to appreciate and validate you. Refer to Chapter 3 and start valuing yourself. You don't have to give something to be loved, appreciated, or valued. You are worthy despite what other people may think. Create a list of things that make you happy and spend time doing these activities. This list could include hobbies, activities like watching movies, or even the foods that you like eating. Whenever you feel upset, or you are struggling to cope, refer to this list and do something that makes you happy.

Key Takeaways

- Self-care is about providing yourself with the love and attention that you always give others.

- It doesn't need to be fancy to be effective.

- Introduce self-care into your life by treating yourself as if you were a child.

- The list of self-care strategies form the foundation of any basic self-care routine.

- Reach out to a therapist or go to group therapy to help yourself stay on track on your recovery journey.

- Use the self-care tips to help you create a personalized self-care plan.

Reflection Activity

Answer the questions below in your notebook.

1. Create a daily schedule that helps you incorporate at least one type of self-care strategy a day. Remember that you can change and alter this schedule as you determine what does and doesn't work for you.

2. Use the activities in this chapter to start incorporating basic self-care into your daily routine.

CHAPTER 7

Being Your Own Woman

Don't sabotage yourself. There are plenty of other people
willing to do that for free.
–Jenny Lawson

The journey to recovery looks different for everyone. These differences originate from how you experience codependency and how it impacts you. You need to tailor your journey to suit your needs and experiences in order to successfully overcome the challenges that you will encounter. I want you to remember something extremely important as you go on your journey: Recovery is a long-term process, and it won't always be easy. As much as you may want to start seeing changes overnight, it will take some time for you to see a positive difference. However, if you continue to work hard, remain persistent, and resilient, then you will start experiencing the benefits of recovery. During your journey you will have bad days. Unfortunately, even people who aren't codependent have bad days. When you struggle, you need to remind yourself that it doesn't mean that you have not made progress. Recovering from codependency isn't easy and problems such as self-sabotage and relapse are challenges that you could face. If you overcome these challenges and continue your journey, you will start experiencing the benefits of your hard work, but you need to be persistent! So what do these benefits look like?

Codependency Recovery in the Long-Term

When you start recovering from codependency, you start living a healthier life. This means that you are learning to cope with, and overcome, challenges by yourself, you are confident in your abilities, and you have learned how to provide yourself with the love and care that you have been lacking in the past. However, recovery is a continuous process. The benefits that you experience from this process will change over time to suit how you are living your life. It's normal to have days where you feel as though you have made no progress, or you feel like you are repeating your codependent behaviors.

Start by taking a breath. Repeat to yourself, "I may be having a bad day (or struggling at the moment), but that won't destroy the progress I have made." Then, you can start using the tools and strategies in the previous chapters to help you resolve your current problem. Start with self-care. Sometimes we feel as though we are making no progress, or slipping into old habits, when all we need to do is take some time to properly care for ourselves.

As you progress on your journey to recovery, you will start discovering who your authentic self is, what she likes, and how to take proper care of her. This is important but it's a slow process. Don't rush it! If you speed up the recovery process, there is the risk that you may become overwhelmed, or even relapse into your codependent behavior. This means that you will have to start the recovery process over again. It isn't anything to be ashamed of. Sometimes it is best to restart the process and use what you previously learned to help you recover from codependency. You need to learn that it's okay to accept your flaws and mistakes without feeling ashamed of them. Many may consider failure a flaw, but it's actually an opportunity for you to learn and grow. Flaws aren't bad, but they are a part of us. To embrace your authentic self is to accept these flaws without conditions. You can't "cure" yourself from codependency. Recovery is a life-long process; however, if you are willing to put in the effort and continue this journey despite the challenges you might face, you will start to see the signs of recovery and benefit from them.

Signs of Codependency Recovery

The way that your life will look while recovering from codependency will differ compared to another woman's. However, there are common signs that you will begin to notice because they will positively impact your life. The list below is not exhaustive as you may see benefits in your life that are not included below. According to Ferguson (1999) and Martin (2020), as you start recovering from codependency, you will:

- Cultivate the ability to validate your own feelings and experiences.

- Begin taking note of the things that you do right, and celebrating these moments.

- Start taking responsibility for your emotions, behavior, and reactions in a situation.

- Celebrate the progress that you make, even if it's small.

- Create realistic expectations for yourself that you have the ability to meet without overwhelming or hurting yourself.

- Stop attempting to meet unrealistic expectations that were set by others and start figuring out what you want and need in your life.

- Cultivate the ability to care for the needs and feelings of others, while respecting their ability to take responsibility and meet their own needs.

- Stop taking responsibility for the lives of others and relinquishing your control over them.

- Have the ability to give because it makes you happy and not because you feel obligated to do it.

- Begin feeling safe and stop sacrificing your identity and mental and physical health for the benefit of others.

- Recognize and acknowledge when you have made a mistake so that you can take responsibility for it.

- When you make a mistake, you no longer feel inadequate. Instead, you accept that mistakes happen and understand that they provide you with the opportunity to learn and grow as a woman.

- Prioritize yourself so that you can provide yourself with the same intense emotional, physical, and spiritual care that you normally give to everyone else.

- Understand that a person's thoughts and opinions about you do not reflect who you are in reality. Instead, it reflects how *they* perceive you.

- Allow yourself to take time to step away from a situation

so that you can calm down and think about what happened. This helps you respond appropriately without hurting yourself or others.

- Know that you do not owe anyone an explanation for your decisions, behavior, or actions. You understand, and have accepted, that you are allowed to do what is best for you without feeling guilty or obligated to explain yourself.

- Step away from a relationship that is unhealthy, codependent, or abusive.

- Respect that other people do have the ability to solve their problems and they need to take responsibility for themselves.

- If you are treated poorly by others, you remove yourself from the situation and speak up to defend yourself.

- Cultivate the ability to take time to rest without feeling guilty.

- Have the skills needed to express your needs and meet them.

- Cultivate a self-awareness that helps you stay in touch with your authentic self.

- Stop trying to prove your worth to others using acts of

service or achievements because you are already worthy.

- You won't always be able to please everyone, and you don't need to.

- Start becoming selective about the opinions that you think should matter to you.

The Challenges That You Will Face During Recovery

While you will start to see the signs of recovery and experience their benefits, you will also face challenges on your journey. The challenges that you face will be unique to you; however, one common challenge that codependent women face is self-sabotage. Self-sabotage is a negative behavior that prevents you from working toward your recovery. In essence, it's self-destructive behavior that makes it difficult for you to make progress during your recovery. This behavior can be dangerous because it may trigger a relapse that causes you to fall back on your codependent tendencies. While this may sound scary, it doesn't mean that you will be stuck as a codependent woman for the rest of your life. It merely means that you will need to restart your recovery process using what you previously learned to help you. But why do you sabotage yourself when you desperately want to recover from codependency?

Reasons for Self-Sabotage

A codependent woman may sabotage herself for a variety of reasons when she starts to recognize her recovery from codependency. These reasons will differ depending on how you experience codependency. This section details the general reasons for self-sabotage; however, you may discover an explanation for why you sabotage yourself that is not included here. In your notebook, make a note of the reasons that you identify with, and provide a short explanation about why you identify with it.

Low Self-Esteem and Self-Worth

Often, problems with one's self-worth and self-esteem can be attributed to the problems you experienced during your childhood—such as trauma or a dysfunctional family dynamic. The problems that occurred during this time negatively impacted your self-image. This makes you vulnerable to self-sabotage because you do not believe that you deserve to be successful or experience good things in your life. This is also called "cognitive dissonance." As human beings, we need our beliefs and values to match our actions. If you believe that you do not deserve to successfully recover from codependency, then you may start to sabotage yourself so that your actions and beliefs can align.

Imposter Syndrome

Issues with low self-esteem and self-worth can also contribute to imposter syndrome. This is when you feel as though you are fooling everyone around you when you are successful. You believe they will discover that you do not actually deserve the success that you have achieved. You are afraid that your achievements will be taken away from you at any moment. Using techniques such as positive affirmations, you need to work on improving your self-esteem and self-worth. You won't see improvements overnight, and you may struggle with your self-esteem throughout the recovery process, but don't let it stop you!

Procrastination

I think many of us are familiar with procrastination. This is a self-sabotaging behavior that occurs when you delay doing what is important to you. You may delay tasks and activities until the last moment because you are afraid of failing, being successful, or disappointing others. You need to be able to identify your fear in order to confront it, determine its validity, and then make a decision on whether you should complete the task or not.

Control

As a codependent woman, you may find that you like to be in control of things. This is actually a normal symptom of codependency; however, it can take the form of a self-sabotaging behavior. Often, when we feel like we will fail at something, we would prefer to have as much control over our failure as possible. This need for control can cause failure because you don't allow yourself to believe the possibility that you will be successful if you let go of your need for control. During your recovery, you may try to control every aspect of it; however, that isn't possible. You have to let go of your need for control in order to make progress on your journey.

Perfectionism

When you are codependent, you may hold yourself to standards that are impossible to reach. This results in setbacks and failures that make you feel guilty, ashamed, and depressed, further preventing your success. You need to learn to let go of your need to be perfect. Lower your expectations for yourself by creating smaller expectations that can be achieved. When you achieve them, celebrate and acknowledge your success. During the recovery process, you might try to perfectly perform every recovery strategy, but recovery isn't about being perfect. Your journey is about making progress that helps you achieve a healthier life where you are happy and have the ability to successfully manage your codependent tendencies.

Familiarity

Human beings like consistency, whether you are codependent or not. However, we often value familiarity above our comfort. This may result in self-sabotaging behavior that prevents us from encountering new things that have risks attached to them. The journey to recovery is full of risks. It might be easier to stay where you are at the expense of your own health and safety, but that doesn't mean that you should do it. Start making small changes. This will help you manage change better because it won't overwhelm you. Once you start getting comfortable again, take the next step on your journey to recovery.

How To Overcome These Challenges

Use the questions in the activity below to help you identify *why* you may be sabotaging yourself. Understanding the reason why is important to being able to successfully overcome these challenges. The steps below form a foundation that you can alter and adjust to suit the unique challenges that you face.

Step 1: Cultivate Awareness

Using techniques such as mindfulness practices (discussed in previous activities) you can become aware of the moments when you start to sabotage yourself. Awareness can help you take away the power that acts of self-sabotage normally have over you. You have to constantly pay attention to identify possible self-sabotage, recognize and acknowledge it, and then label the type of sabotage that occurs.

Step 2: Identify the Cause

Now, you have to understand *why* you are sabotaging yourself in order to be able to overcome it. Reflect on your past experiences where you may have sabotaged yourself. Do you notice a pattern, a specific emotion, or perhaps a common event that triggered your self-sabotage?

Step 3: Challenge It

Then, determine whether your reason for sabotaging yourself is logical. In other words, ask yourself if you are sabotaging yourself to prevent yourself from entering a dangerous situation, or are you sabotaging yourself because you are afraid?

Step 4: Let Go of Perceived Outcomes

You have to let go of how you think something should happen. Reality often doesn't turn out how we want it too, and that's okay. You need to learn to accept that and embrace it otherwise you will be disappointed, feel ashamed, or feel as though you failed because the situation didn't turn out exactly how you hoped it would. Instead, take small steps toward overcoming challenges so that you don't overwhelm yourself. Actively decide not to participate in self-destructive behaviors, and replace them with a healthier behavior, like mindfulness meditation or going for a walk.

Step 5: Don't Try to Be Perfect

Recovery is about making positive progress on your journey, not about being perfect. You can do something perfectly without having made any progress and staying stuck in your codependent ways. Remember that small improvements can help you reach your goal and should be celebrated.

Key Takeaways

- Your journey will look different to the journeys of other women.

- Recovery isn't easy.

- The benefits of recovery will change as your lifestyle changes for the better.

- The signs of codependency recovery will look different for every woman.

- You will experience unique challenges during your

journey to recovery; however, self-sabotage is a common challenge.

- There are many reasons for self-sabotage, and you need to identify them in order to overcome them.

Activity

Answer the list of questions below to gain better insight into why you may currently be preventing yourself from working toward codependency recovery. You can use this list of questions every time your tendency to self-sabotage is triggered.

1. Does your current behavior align with your goal to recover from codependency?

2. If you answered "no," identify what is preventing you from reaching your goal.

3. Does your behavior align with your current values and beliefs? If you answered 'no,' please explain why in detail.

4. When you make progress working toward recovery, do you feel uncomfortable? Please explain why you think you feel this way, in detail.

5. If you identified a fear in any of the above questions,

please state what you are afraid of and explain why you are afraid. This will help you start to overcome your fear.

6. When you achieve success on your journey to recovery, do you believe that you don't deserve your success? Explain why in detail.

7. Reflect on your answers and use the section on how you can overcome challenges to help you confront your fears and overcome the obstacles that are preventing you from progressing on your journey to recovery.

CHAPTER 8

Dating Yourself

In order to create the relationship that you're dreaming of you need to first start from the inside and work your way out.
–Dr. Jeanine Staples

The relationship that you have with yourself is the most important relationship that you will experience in your life. While it is nice to make friends and have healthy relationships with others, you don't need them in order to have meaningful experiences. As a codependent woman, you already struggle with putting yourself first because you are prone to prioritizing others. By cultivating a healthy relationship with yourself, you make yourself a priority and improve your well-being. Codependency tangles your identity with your partner's. It becomes difficult to know what you like even though you can name the details about why your partner hates a specific movie. As you start on your journey to recover from codependency, you may feel lost because you don't know who you are without your partner or relationship. The recovery process may even seem intimidating because you feel like a stranger to yourself. You might struggle with independence and low self-esteem because you relied on your relationship to provide you with validation and direction. To remedy this, you have to allow yourself to get to know the "real" you—even if she is a stranger. However, it might make you more prone to self-sabotage because you are afraid of the unknown, even if the unknown is you.

What Does "Dating Yourself" Mean?

The one person who spends the most time with you is you. On the journey to recovery, you have to learn how to enjoy your own company. This can improve your self-esteem and teach you how to love yourself. You can also use your alone time to get to know your authentic self better. Romantic love is often seen as more important than self-love in many cultures. However, learning to love who you are as an individual, in spite of your flaws and mistakes, is one of the most important things that you can do while recovering from codependency. But why is this so important? Well, besides the obvious reasons like boosting your confidence and ensuring that you take care of your needs, self-love can be considered the key to codependency recovery. The thing is, in order to have a healthy, loving relationship with someone else, you first need to have a healthy and loving relationship with yourself. This type of relationship is commonly known as "dating yourself."

Simply put, "dating yourself" is a type of self-care where you learn how to feel confident and secure in who you are as a woman, develop a sense of independence that allows you to have fun doing things by yourself, as well as teaching you how to be comfortable when you are alone. You learn that you deserve respect and learn how to give yourself that respect without relying on others. This helps you decide how you want to be treated by others. Learning about who you are as a woman can help you discover what you really want from a relationship, including how you deserve to be treated.

Dating yourself looks different for everyone because different things make us happy. What matters is that you allow yourself to enjoy your company, learn more about the woman that has been in hiding all these years, and care for her in a suitable manner. Dating yourself can be daunting in the beginning, especially if you struggle with low self-esteem, but it's an ongoing journey that will benefit you, allowing you to be happy and free to be your authentic self. Before you start the process of dating yourself, answer the questions below in your notebook. This will provide you with a starting point to help you understand what you want out of this process.

What Is Preventing You From Loving Yourself?

As a codependent woman, you probably struggle to provide yourself with the same love and acceptance that you give to others. This can create a need for external validation, difficulty believing in yourself, negative self-talk, and a belief that you *need* to be in a relationship in order to function. The best way to overcome this is to purposefully take time for yourself to get comfortable with who you are, and realize that you can be happy on your own.

What Do You Want to Add to Your Relationship With Yourself?

Through the process of getting to know yourself, you have the opportunity to reflect on what you want from a relationship with yourself. This may include things like improving your self-esteem, learning how to validate yourself, and understanding that you deserve to be treated well without having to earn it. This gives you the opportunity to focus on your personal goals, take part in new experiences, and discover what makes you happy.

How Much Time Can You Dedicate to Yourself?

Dating yourself will take time and effort. However, if you are willing to work hard and tailor dating yourself to suit your lifestyle, then you will learn how to be successfully independent and accept yourself for who you are. Prioritizing yourself is important on the journey to codependency recovery. After prioritizing everyone else for so long, it's now time to put yourself first.

Why Is Dating Yourself Important?

Relationships can be enjoyable, but you don't need to have a partner in order to be happy. Dating yourself teaches you how to successfully care for your emotional, mental, and physical well-being in a way that helps you thrive on your own. It has a number of benefits, from learning how to prioritize yourself to understanding that you don't need another person to provide you with love and care to be happy. These benefits will differ depending on the life you lead, but that doesn't make them any less valuable.

The Benefits of Dating Yourself

You can avoid codependent relationships by understanding yourself better and learning what you are capable of on your own. It will also help you avoid relapsing into codependent behaviors if you are triggered. Being on your own can be fun. You learn how to provide yourself with attention, respect, and validation in a way that is meaningful to you. You will need to be patient and remain persistent in practicing this strategy if you want to experience each of these benefits. The section that follows provides you with some of the benefits that dating yourself can bring you; however, this list is not exhaustive.

Improve Your Confidence

As you get to know yourself better, you move out of your comfort zone. This can feel awkward and may even be scary, but the sense of accomplishment that you feel afterwards is worth it. Your confidence increases when you learn how to make yourself happy. This helps you feel comfortable doing things by yourself. In turn, it benefits your self-esteem and teaches you to value who you are. You will start feeling more comfortable going out into the world on your own, taking yourself to dinner, going to an art class, or simply enjoying your company as you take a walk in the park.

Cultivate Self-Awareness

When you start to uncover your true self, you have to take the time to get to know her properly—just like you would with someone that you just met. Dating yourself helps you to discover what *you* like and dislike, your passions, favorite food and music, as well as a number of other things. Learning about yourself and who you are as a unique individual helps you cultivate a sense of self-awareness that is important in developing and maintaining healthy boundaries and making decisions that will benefit you.

Teach You How to Love Yourself

You might avoid getting to know yourself because you are afraid of spending time alone with this woman that you know nothing about. It's almost like spending time with a stranger, except you can hear her thoughts. I'll be honest, it is terrifying. However, that doesn't mean you should allow it to hold you back. When you take the time to get to know yourself, without judgment, and start accepting who you are—weird thoughts and imperfections included—you will realize that you are pretty amazing. Learning to enjoy your own company is the first step to accepting yourself without any conditions. This will help you develop a love for who you really are.

Personal Growth

Dating yourself teaches you how to grow as an independent woman. When you prioritize yourself, you purposefully create the time to work on your goals, reflect on your personal needs, and identify why you have a strong need for companionship. Personal growth involves getting to know who you are on a personal level, often in a way that no one else does—or ever will—know you. This improves your confidence, sense of identity, self-awareness, and self-esteem.

Improve Your Relationships

Dating yourself helps you gain an understanding of what you deserve in a healthy relationship. The self-respect that you develop during this process ensures that you stand up for yourself in your relationships, and prevents you from allowing your partner to treat you badly. Additionally, having a healthy relationship with yourself helps you learn how to have a healthy relationship with your partner.

Independence

To be truly happy as an independent woman, you need to learn that you don't need someone else to help you accomplish things. You learn how to accept yourself for who you are, take responsibility for your actions and emotions, and build healthy boundaries and uphold them. Not only does this help you grow as a woman, but it also allows you to enjoy your life and take proper care of yourself to ensure your mental and physical well-being.

How to Date Yourself

Learning how to date yourself is important and quite simple.

Instead of planning a date for a significant other, you are planning it for yourself. The process is the same, except you don't have to wait for your partner to arrive. I previously mentioned that dating yourself is a type of self-care. This is important to note because you may put off taking yourself on dates because you feel like you are wasting your time. The truth is that self-care is a productive behavior. Codependency drains your energy and negatively impacts your physical and mental well-being. Additionally, remaining constantly 'productive' does the same thing, but dating yourself can help you take care of yourself.

What Does Dating Yourself Entail?

Well, you would take yourself on dates that you want to go on. These dates could involve going out to the movies or the park. You can stay at home and watch your favorite movie, practice positive self-talk, or cook for yourself. You don't need to spend money to date yourself. Even if you do spend money on yourself, you shouldn't do anything that you can't afford. Dating yourself is about doing things that make you happy and contribute to your emotional, mental, and physical well-being. You can try new things or take part in activities that have made you happy in the past. Try to be receptive and open to new things as you go on this journey. Dating yourself will teach you a lot about who you are, while also helping you take care of yourself. The only thing you need to do is ensure that you have fun while you do it. So how do you make time to date yourself?

Making Time to Date Yourself

Schedule Time in Your Calendar for a Date

You will need to look at your schedule and decide on a specific date every month, or a specific weekday, to go on your date. You can even set a specific time during the day for your date. It's important that you remain firm about your decision and prioritize yourself during this time.

Put Yourself First

Always make sure that you are prioritizing yourself in your daily life. Caring for yourself doesn't happen only during your dates. This could take the form of saying "no."

Incorporate Self-Care

On your dates, you can include activities that involve some form of self-care, like positive self-talk. This will allow you to experience the benefits of self-care and dating yourself simultaneously.

Plan Your Dates in Advance

Plan your dates, in detail, a few weeks before they happen so that you don't back out at the last minute.

Start Journaling

In your notebook, write about what you expect from dating yourself. You can detail how you feel before, during, and after your date, as well as what you hope to learn. This will help you become more aware of yourself and keep track of your personal growth.

Embrace the Excitement

Allow yourself to look forward to spending your time alone doing something that you enjoy or have been wanting to do for years. Get excited because you are looking forward to having fun!

Date Ideas

There are numerous date ideas available on the internet. Everyone has a different idea of fun and relaxation, so the perfect date will look different between individuals. In your notebook, make a list of possible date ideas that will help you plan your dates in advance. Create a list of things that you currently enjoy doing. Then create a list of things that you would like to do. You can also set aside a section for new ideas. While numerous date ideas exist, you can use the list below to help you create your list of date ideas.

- Have a movie night at home.

- Go out to the theater to see that new movie you have been looking forward to.

- Take yourself out for dinner or stay at home and cook for yourself using a new recipe.

- Dress up for yourself, even if you don't go out for your date.

- Practice positive affirmations in front of your mirror.

- Listen to your favorite music and dance around your home.

- Buy yourself flowers.

- Write yourself love letters where you talk positively about yourself and your achievements.

- Take yourself out for coffee.

- Visit your local museum.

- Have a picnic in the park.

- Go on holiday to somewhere you have always wanted to visit.

Key Takeaways

- You can meet your authentic self and get to know her using a method called "dating yourself."

- Self-love (one of the benefits of dating yourself) is important for successfully recovering from codependency.

- Dating yourself helps you develop a reference for what you want in a healthy relationship.

- Dating yourself is about having fun and allowing yourself to grow.

- You don't need to complicate dating yourself in order to have fun and benefit from it.

Activity

Answer the questions that follow in your notebook.

1. Write down your dream date in detail.

2. Identify the different elements and activities involved in your dream date. Use these elements to create a custom list of date ideas.

3. Using one element per date, plan a series of dates for the next month.

4. Start going on dates with yourself. At the end of each date, journal about it. In each journal entry, you should reflect on how the date made you feel, whether you enjoyed yourself, if there was anything you wished you had done on your date, and what you learned during your date.

CHAPTER 9

Maintaining Interdependence

All have their worth and each contributes to the worth of the others.

–J.R.R. Tolkien

One of the many reasons for starting the recovery process, and putting in the hard work, is to get to the point in your journey where you are comfortable developing a romantic relationship with someone. Codependency negatively impacts many aspects of your life, often resulting in codependent relationships that hurt both partners. You may even avoid romantic relationships for fear of relapsing into your codependent tendencies. But you shouldn't have to live your whole life afraid of relationships. If you work to develop a healthier relationship that has interdependent characteristics, you and your partner will flourish and grow together. Although, cultivating an interdependent relationship requires that you first learn how to be independent.

When you began your journey to recovery, we focused on identifying the origins of your codependency, and learning to rely on, and care for, yourself using methods like self-care. These steps, and the strategies that they incorporate, all aimed to provide you with the ability to develop the independence that you need to develop a healthy relationship with yourself, as well as with a potential romantic partner. As a codependent woman, you struggle to receive gifts, acts of service, or accept love from your partner. Once you learn how to provide yourself with love, validation, and acceptance through independence, you will reach the point in your journey where you'll be able to accept these actions from a partner without ending up in a codependent relationship.

What Is Interdependence?

An interdependent relationship is when both partners recognize the value of their mutually respectful emotional and physical bond that they share. Each partner is able to maintain their independence and boundaries, while also feeling safe enough to be vulnerable around their partner, both physically and emotionally. Both partners are able to dedicate time to their relationship with each other and themselves without feeling guilty. If conflict arises in their relationship, both partners communicate with each other so that they can work together to solve their problems without hurting their partner or relationship.

Codependency vs Interdependence

After being codependent for so long, one thing is for certain—you don't want to enter into a codependent relationship again. You should try to cultivate interdependence in your relationship instead. Interdependence is not the exact opposite of codependency; however, you can use it as a guide for creating a healthier romantic relationship. While interdependence is great, how exactly does it compare to codependence?

Codependence

When you first enter a relationship, it's normal to want to spend as much time as you can with your partner, but this can create problems like codependence that create an unbalanced relationship. This isn't healthy or sustainable. A codependent relationship negatively impacts every part of your life. You start losing your identity, feel resentful toward your partner, or solve problems at your own expense. This isn't fair to either of you and can severely impact your self-worth and self-esteem.

Interdependence

When you cultivate interdependence in your relationship, you encourage a balance between the roles that you and your partner play. Through clear communication, you are able to create clearly defined boundaries that are healthy and protect the independence of each partner. This allows both of you to feel safe and secure in your partnership, even when issues arise. If a problem does occur, both partners work to resolve it in a way that doesn't negatively impact one of the partners. It strengthens your relationship instead. You know that while you have the freedom and independence to pursue your own goals, your partner will be there if you need them, and you are secure in this knowledge that you aren't alone.

The Benefits of an Interdependent Relationship

There are numerous benefits to cultivating an interdependent relationship, especially if you struggle with codependent behaviors. Interdependence helps you to build a strong and healthy relationship that positively impacts your life. The benefits of interdependence vary; however, some of the more common benefits include

Not Giving Up Your Dreams

Codependence prevents you from focusing on your own goals because your time and energy is being used to support your partner and help them reach their goals at the expense of your own. Interdependence allows you to continue making progress with your self-care and allows you to take time to continue dating yourself. It helps you separate your personal and professional life from your relationship in a healthy way that doesn't make you feel guilty for taking time to yourself. At the end of the day, you come back to your partner and share what you did and learned during the day. This allows you to grow together.

Healthy Boundaries

Healthy boundaries will allow you to maintain your independence and identity, while respecting your and your partner's needs. This helps you to maintain your sense of self-worth and encourages you to take responsibility for your actions and behaviors without fear of judgment or damaging consequences, like abusive behavior.

Safety and Security

Respecting your boundaries, communicating without fear of judgment, and the creation of healthy boundaries helps develop a space in the relationship where both partners feel comfortable being vulnerable around each other. This encourages you to be your authentic self without fearing that you will scare your partner or hurt them.

Communication

Open and honest communication is important in any

relationship. In a codependent relationship, open communication is lacking because one partner is afraid of being honest or expressing their opinion to their partner. However, an interdependent relationship encourages both partners to express their opinions and communicate because the other partner will actively listen without judgment. You don't fear being rejected or punished for what you have to say. Instead, you look forward to hearing your partner's thoughts or receiving their support when you are struggling. This also ensures that any problems that arise in your relationship are appropriately dealt with without hurting either partner.

Listening

While feeling comfortable communicating is important, it's also important that you actively listen to your partner when they are communicating with you. Your partner would do the same for you in an interdependent relationship. When your partner actively listens to you, you feel heard and encouraged to continue sharing your problems, thoughts, and feelings with them. You also feel supported because your partner gains insight into how you are feeling and what is happening in your personal and professional life. In turn, your partner will feel the same way when you listen to them.

Saying "No"

In a codependent relationship, you don't feel comfortable

saying "no," or you may struggle with it. Being able to say "no" is extremely important for your mental and physical well-being. In an interdependent relationship, the mutual respect between you and your partner, and your confidence in your self-worth, means that you feel comfortable saying "no" to your partner without fear of unfair repercussions that are common in codependent relationships.

Independence

When you have a healthy relationship with your partner, you feel comfortable dedicating time to yourself and time with your partner without feeling guilty. Personal time is extremely important—especially if you are recovering from codependency—because it allows you to practice self-care, work on your goals, or just enjoy your time to yourself without having to worry about anyone else.

Building and Maintaining an Interdependent Relationship

As you go on your journey of recovering from codependency, you will reach a stage where you may want to enter into a new romantic relationship. Whether you are ready for a relationship will depend on you and how confident you feel about pursuing a relationship with someone. However, you may be concerned that your relationship will become codependent, or you may want to develop an interdependent relationship from the beginning. Either way, when you enter into a new relationship, you need to use every skill that you have previously learned in this book to assist you and prevent you from relapsing into codependent behaviors. Some additional tips that you can use when you enter into a new relationship include:

Know Who You Are

You need to know who you are as an independent woman before you enter into a relationship. Although, this doesn't mean that you won't have the opportunity for personal growth as your relationship progresses. Essentially, knowing who you are is important for preventing you from losing your identity and independence to your relationship.

Take Time for Self-Reflection

Actively dedicate time for personal reflection. You can use the mindfulness meditation activities in the previous chapters to help you. Being aware of your mind and body will help you notice if your codependent tendencies have been triggered so that you can work on managing them before they start negatively impacting you and your relationship.

Take Personal Time

At the beginning of the relationship, you and your partner need to ensure that you both have the space to safely develop as individuals, as well as partners. This involves things like learning to communicate openly and listening to each other without fear of judgment.

Stand Up for Yourself

It's important that you stand up for yourself in your relationship. Don't tolerate unhealthy, manipulative, or abusive behavior. Your partner may not be doing it intentionally, but you are the one that suffers. Communicate openly and honestly with your partner about how you feel when they talk to you in a specific way or mistreat you. Then, decide whether you want to work together to resolve the issue or end your relationship. You have worked so hard to recover from codependency to get to this point, don't allow your partner to take that from you because they aren't ready to be in a relationship.

Maintain Your Identity and Independence

According to Clarke (2018), you and your partner can use the following strategies to help you maintain your independence and sense of self as you start your relationship. You should continue to practice these strategies even as your relationship progresses. These strategies include:

- being your authentic self and not hiding who you are.

- knowing what you like and dislike.

- understanding what matters to you.

- saying "no."

- being able to ask for what you need.

- taking time to work on your hobbies and goals.

- always being mindful of your values and beliefs, and upholding them.

Key Takeaways

- You first have to learn how to be independent before you can have an interdependent relationship with someone else.

- Interdependent relationships are healthier than codependent relationships.

- There are a variety of benefits to developing a healthy, interdependent relationship.

- The point at which you are ready for a romantic relationship, while on your journey to recovery, will be different compared to someone else. Don't rush it. If you don't feel ready to pursue a romantic relationship, then wait until you are ready.

Activity

Answer the following questions in your notebook.

1. Explain why you do or do not want to be in a healthy romantic relationship in detail. You can use this question to help you decide whether you are ready to enter into a relationship or not.

2. Identify whether *you* would prefer to pursue a codependent or interdependent relationship? Explain why.

3. Describe what your dream relationship looks like in detail.

4. When you are considering pursuing a relationship, answer the questions above and reflect on them to help you ensure that you are entering into a relationship because you *want* to and not because you are feeling lonely.

Conclusion

It is good to have an end to journey toward; but it is the
journey that matters, in the end.
—Ursula K. Le Guin

Recovering from codependency is possible, but it won't happen overnight. Although, being able to meet your true self as you go on this journey of recovery will be worth it. As a codependent woman, you have survived the pain and trauma that you experienced in the only way you could. Being codependent isn't anything to be ashamed of, but it's important that you are persistent on your journey to recovery so that you can live a life where you have healthy relationships and take care of yourself so that the woman that you truly are is nurtured and allowed to grow without fear or pain.

What Did I Cover?

I covered a variety of information related to codependency, along with tips and strategies that you can use to help you work on your recovery. It's important that you approach the information with an open mind and integrate the information in a way that suits your lifestyle. This will help you create a recovery strategy that is tailored to your unique experience of codependency, as well as your lifestyle. Use the activities that were included throughout each chapter to help you put them into practice.

Chapter 1 explained that when a woman is codependent, she often has low self-esteem and a need for external validation that develops into unhealthy, dependent behaviors that impact both her and her partner. Codependency itself is experienced differently by everyone, but it has many common traits that you can use to determine whether you are codependent. While understanding what codependency is is important, you also need to understand how your codependent tendencies originated. In Chapter 2, you learned that codependency often results from traumatic experiences in your childhood. As a child, you didn't have the experience, skills, or resources to be able to successfully cope with the trauma that you experienced. These consequences manifested as codependent behaviors and relationships. Traumatic situations created feelings of helplessness. What is important here is that you recognize and acknowledge the trauma you experienced and continue to work toward recovery.

The traditional role of a woman as the "giver" in a family dynamic—as explained in Chapter 3—can result in excessive giving, nurturing, caring, and helpful behavior that negatively impacts you. It can result in patterns of codependency that you use to protect yourself and cope, but the consequences may manifest as a need for external validation. External validation is an extremely unhealthy behavior that may make you feel guilty, unworthy, or ashamed because you have to rely heavily on another person. However, you can use the strategies that were discussed in this chapter to help you learn how to validate yourself in a healthy way.

Codependency also impacts your relationships. You can use Chapter 4 to better understand how codependency affects your thoughts and behavior in your relationship. Your style of attachment is developed in childhood. It's an instinctual behavior, but you can use it to help you reflect on your relationships and understand why certain problems—like codependency—develop. The thought of being alone creates feelings of loneliness, dejection, and worthlessness. To protect yourself, you stay in an unhealthy relationship, but there are numerous ways to cope with leaving a codependent relationship.

The victim mentality is common among codependent women,

especially if they feel resentful toward their partner. Chapter 5 explains how this mindset manifests from a belief that you are the victim, no matter the situation you are in. It makes it difficult for you to take responsibility, so you blame your unhappiness on others, but you can recover! Using strategies like mindfulness activities, you can take note of your thoughts and feelings so that you can start making changes using techniques like positive affirmations. You have to stand up for yourself and see yourself as a woman who is valuable so that you can start taking responsibility for your life and acknowledge your true identity.

Taking proper care of yourself is something many codependent women struggle with. Chapter 6 discussed basic self-care and the strategies that you could use to help you feel less guilty about taking time to care for yourself. Self-care may not be glamorous, but it will help you restore your energy and take the time to meet your needs. You will learn what makes you happy, as well as who you are without codependency. Self-care looks different for every woman. You have to create a routine that suits your lifestyle and needs. You can start this process by learning how to meet your basic needs and moving on from there. It's normal to feel guilty when you start practicing self-care; after all, you are used to caring for others, not yourself. It's important that you are compassionate to yourself and your emotions, but continue to practice self-care despite feelings of guilt.

Self-care helps you to take the first steps to cultivating your independence as a woman. Chapter 7 discusses what your life will look like as you start to recover from codependency. You will meet your true self, learn how to care for and nurture her, and how to maintain your independence. Although you will also face challenges like self-sabotage on your journey to recovery, you can overcome them if you are patient, persistent, and believe in your abilities as a woman.

Through strategies like "dating yourself," discussed in Chapter 8, you learned how to get to know yourself. By literally dating yourself, you create the opportunity to understand who you are as a woman, what you need and want in life, as well as how you can grow and pursue your goals. Your relationship with yourself is more important than any other relationship that you will have because you cannot expect to have a healthy relationship with someone else if you cannot have a healthy relationship with yourself.

A healthy relationship with a partner is also called an "interdependent relationship." Chapter 9 explained what an interdependent relationship is, how it compares to an unhealthy and codependent relationship, and how it can benefit you as a codependent woman. There are numerous benefits, but an interdependent relationship is valuable because it allows you and your partner to grow as individuals, as well as a couple. But you have to put in the work to build and maintain a healthy relationship with your partner.

What Did You Learn?

After reading this book, you will have a thorough understanding of what codependency is, how it originates and impacts your life, as well as how you can recover from it. On your journey to recovery, you will begin to heal from your childhood trauma and learn who you truly are as a woman. This will help you better understand how you can nurture your true self so that she may grow and flourish, whether she is single or in a relationship.

Call to Action

You now have a foundation on which to build your personalized recovery plan. It's important that you understand that while being codependent is nothing to be ashamed of, it is now time for you to use what you have learned and go—not only a journey of recovery—but on one of discovery.

Thank You

Before you leave, I'd just like to say, thank you so much for purchasing my book.

I spent many days and nights working on this book so I could finally put this in your hands.

So, before you leave, I'd like to ask you a small favor.

Would you please consider posting a review on the platform? Your reviews are one of the best ways to support indie authors like me, and every review counts.

Your feedback will allow me to continue writing books just like this one, so let me know if you enjoyed it and why. I read every review and I would love to hear from you. Simply visit the link below to leave a review.

References

Bardo, N. (2021, August 11). How to date yourself: 30 Things to do alone. *It's All You Boo*. https://itsallyouboo.com/how-to-date-yourself-30-things-to-do-alone/

Beattie, M. (1992). *Codependent no more: how to stop controlling others and start caring for yourself.* Taylor and Francis.

Beattie, M. (2022). The language of letting go: Hazelden meditation series. In Simon and Schuster (Ed.), *Lib Quotes*. https://libquotes.com/melody-beattie/quote/lbq9r8t (Original work published 2009)

The Best Self. (2020, July 31). *73 (Most relatable) quotes on self sabotage*. Becoming The Best Self. https://becomingthebestself.com/quotes-on-self-sabotage/

Body Mind Spirit. (2014, February 20). *Codependency: What is it and who am I?* Body Mind Spirit.

https://www.bodymindspiritonline.com/codependency-relationships/

Burn, S. M. (2017). Are women more codependent than men? *Psychology* *Today.* https://www.psychologytoday.com/us/blog/presence-mind/201709/are-women-more-codependent-men

Burns, S. (2016, April 29). *10 Inspirational quotes for a happy dating life!* Samantha Burns: Marriage Counselor and Dating Coach. http://www.lovesuccessfully.com/articles/inspirational-quotes-for-a-happy-dating-life

Clarke, J. (2019). *Interdependence can build a lasting and safe relationship.* Very Well Mind. https://www.verywellmind.com/how-to-build-a-relationship-based-on-interdependence-4161249

Cox, J. (2022, July 21). *Leaning into recovery from codependency.* Psych Central. https://psychcentral.com/relationships/recovery-from-codependency

D, A. (2022, January 7). *Understanding interdependence versus codependency.* Healthy Huemans. https://healthyhuemans.com/interdependence-vs-codependency/

Dahunsi, L. (2021, October 20). *Book summary: You're not crazy—you're codependent by Jeanette Elisabeth Menter.* Lanre Dahunsi. https://lanredahunsi.com/book-summary-youre-not-crazy-youre-codependent-by-jeanette-elisabeth-menter/

Dee, M. (2021, December 9). End the vicious cycle of people pleasing (and seeking external validation). *Femmena*. https://www.thefemmena.com/blog/self-development-end-the-vicious-cycle-of-people-pleasing-and-seeking-validation

Dominica. (2022, February 9). *How codependency, victim mentality and addiction are connected and helpful ways to heal.* Daily Motivation. https://www.dailymotivation.site/how-codependency-victim-mentality-addiction-are-connected-helpful-ways-to-heal/

Ellis, M. E. (2020, August 14). How trauma can result in codependency. *Bright Quest Treatment Centers*. https://www.brightquest.com/blog/how-trauma-can-result-in-codependency/

Farris, M. (2019, September 16). How to embrace self-care when you're codependent. *Counseling Recovery*. https://www.counselingrecovery.com/blog-san-jose/self-care-for-codependents

Ferguson, P. L. (1999). *What does recovery from codependency look like?* Peggyferguson.com. http://www.peggyferguson.com/userfiles/10846/file/NewPDFSw_CartButtons/

Fields, B. (2022). *Why people self-sabotage.* Very Well Mind. https://www.verywellmind.com/why-people-self-sabotage-and-how-to-stop-it-5207635

Finn, A., and Alder, S. L. (2022, March 5). *80 Dignity quotes to inspire positive change in your life.* Quote Ambition. https://www.quoteambition.com/dignity-quotes/

Gate House. (2020, March 3). *5 Reasons why codependency and addiction go hand in hand.* Gate House Treatment. https://www.gatehousetreatment.com/codependency-and-addiction/

Gould, W. R. (2020). *What is codependency?* Very Well Mind. https://www.verywellmind.com/what-is-codependency-5072124

Grey, S. (2016, March 14). *Self-sabotage and codependency.* Esteemology. https://esteemology.com/self-sabotage-and-codependency/

Hendriksen, E. (2017). Why do we self-sabotage? *Psychology Today.* https://www.psychologytoday.com/us/blog/how-be-yourself/201710/why-do-we-self-sabotage

Hull, M. (2022, May 26). *Codependency facts and statistics.* The Recovery Village. https://www.therecoveryvillage.com/mental-health/codependency/codependency-statistics/

Hussain, S. (2020). *Red Sugar, No More.* Independently Published.

Jones, H. (2020). *How do I know if I'm in a codependent relationship?* Very Well Health. https://www.verywellhealth.com/codependency-5093171

Juster, N., Feiffer, J., and Sendak, M. (2015). *The phantom tollbooth.* Alfred A. Knopf.

Kholghi, B. (2022, February 5). *11 Ways to stop depending on external validation.* Coaching Online. https://www.coaching-online.org/external-validation/

Khoshaba, D. (2013, July 21). *The codependent woman.* Psychology in Everyday Life. http://www.psychologyineverydaylife.net/2013/07/21/the-codependent-woman/

Kitching, A. (2019). *The quote archive: Forgive yourself for the survival patterns and traits you picked up while enduring trauma.* Tiny Buddha. https://tinybuddha.com/wisdom-quotes/forgive-yourself-for-not-knowing-better-at-the-time/

Kristenson, S. (2022, February 2). *50 Affirmations for codependents to help with recovery.* Happier Human. https://www.happierhuman.com/affirmations-codependents/

Lamberti, A. (2019, July 31). When you struggle with codependency: 5 crucial self-care strategies. *Ashleigh Lamberti Psychotherapist.* https://www.sbcounselor.com/blog/2019/7/30/when-you-struggle-with-codependency-5-crucial-self-care-strategies

Lancer, D. (2016a). *Goals of recovery from codependency.* Dummies. https://www.dummies.com/article/body-mind-spirit/emotional-health-psychology/psychology/diagnoses/codependency/goals-of-recovery-from-codependency-144327/

Lancer, D. (2016b, May). *Trauma and codependency.* Codependency. https://whatiscodependency.com/trauma-and-codependency/

Lancer, D. (2021, May 13). *Steps to codependency recovery*. Different Brains. https://www.differentbrains.org/steps-to-codependency-recovery/

Le Guin, U. K. (1976). *Hainish cycle. 06 : The left hand of darkness*. Ace Books.

Martin, S. (2017, June 19). A guide to self-care for codependents and those who struggle with self-care. *Psych Central*. https://psychcentral.com/blog/imperfect/2017/06/a-guide-to-self-care-for-codependents-and-those-who-struggle-with-self-care

Martin, S. (2020a, January 10). Why it's so hard to end a codependent relationship. *Psych Central*. https://psychcentral.com/blog/imperfect/2020/01/why-its-so-hard-to-end-a-codependent-relationship

Martin, S. (2020b, June 4). 27 Signs that you're recovering from codependency. *Psych Central*. https://psychcentral.com/blog/imperfect/2020/06/27-signs-that-youre-recovering-from-codependency

Martin, S. (2020c, September 18). *Parentified child: When a child has to act like an adult*. Live Well with Sharon Martin. https://www.livewellwithsharonmartin.com/parentified-child/

Mathers, C. (2021, April 16). *5 Ways to take responsibility for your actions (and life)*. Develop Good Habits. https://www.developgoodhabits.com/take-responsibility/

Merriam-Webster. (n.d.-a). Codependency. In the *Merriam-Webster Dictionary*. Retrieved August 1, 2022, from https://www.merriam-webster.com/dictionary/codependency

Merriam-Webster. (n.d.-b). Victim mentality. In the *Merriam-Webster Dictionary*. Retrieved August 12, 2022, from https://www.merriam-webster.com/dictionary/victim%20mentality

Merriam-Webster. (2018). Self-Care. In the *Merriam-Webster Dictionary*. https://www.merriam-webster.com/dictionary/self-care

Morin, A. (2020). *How to stop being codependent*. Very Well Mind. https://www.verywellmind.com/what-s-the-best-codependency-treatment-5070487

Munoz, A. (2021, May 5). *How do you overcome codependency? A therapist's guide*. Mindbodygreen Relationships. https://www.mindbodygreen.com/0-21115/i-used-to-be-codependent-heres-how-i-stay-true-to-myself-in-relationships.html

Psychology Today Staff. (2019). *Codependency*. Psychology Today. https://www.psychologytoday.com/us/basics/codependency

Rosenberg, R. (2021, May 9). *5 Types of codependency and codependent personalities*. The Minds Journal. https://themindsjournal.com/types-codependency-personality/

Scott, S. J. (2017a, June 29). *71 Mindfulness Exercises for Living in the Present Moment*. Develop Good Habits. https://www.developgoodhabits.com/mindfulness-exercises/

Scott, S. J. (2017b, July 20). *What Is Mindfulness? (Includes Five Exercises Increase Mindfulness in Your Life)*. Develop Good Habits. https://www.developgoodhabits.com/what_is_mindfulness/

Seeking Serotonin. (2022). *How to start dating yourself (the ultimate guide)*. Seeking Serotonin. https://seekingserotonin.com/how-to-start-dating-yourself/

Selva, J. (2018, February 9). *Codependency: What are the signs and how to overcome it*. Positive Psychology. https://positivepsychology.com/codependency-definition-signs-worksheets/

Smith, K. (2022, May 20). *Codependency versus interdependency*. Psych Central. https://psychcentral.com/lib/codependency-vs-interdependency#defining-them

Sosnoski, K. (2021, September 30). *Childhood trauma and codependency: Is there a link?* Psych Central. https://psychcentral.com/lib/trauma-and-codependency

Tolkien, C, and Tolkien, J.R.R. (2002). *The Silmarillion*. Ballantine Books.

United We Care. (2022, January 18). Understanding interdependence relationship: How to identify for yourself. *United We Care*. https://www.unitedwecare.com/understanding-interdependence-relationship-how-to-identify-for-yourself/

Wasielewski, S. (2021, February 5). 7 Reasons why dating yourself is important for personal growth (and how to do it!). *Skinny Fit.* https://blog.skinnyfit.com/dating-yourself/

WebMD Editorial Contributors. (2020, November 24). *Signs of codependency.* WebMD. https://www.webmd.com/mental-health/signs-codependency

Women's Recovery. (2020, March 19). Codependency: The warped relationship that feeds addiction. *Women's Recovery.* https://www.womensrecovery.com/womens-rehab-blog/codependency-supports-substance-abuse/

Wood, K. M. (2022, June 13). *How to treat codependency: CBT and codependency.* Confidently Authentic. https://confidentlyauthentic.com/cbt-and-codependency/

www.ingramcontent.com/pod-product-compliance
Lightning Source LLC
Chambersburg PA
CBHW031522120626
46545CB00005B/1964